Alone with the President

ALONE WITH THE PRESIDENT

John Strausbaugh

BLAST BOOKS
NEW YORK

LIBRARY OF CONGRESS CATALOGING-IN-PUBLICATION DATA

Strausbaugh, John.
    Alone with the President / John Strausbaugh. — 1st ed.
      p. cm.
    Includes bibliographical references.
    ISBN 0-922233-10-1 : — ISBN 09-22233-09-8 (pbk.) :
    1. Presidents—United States—Public opinion. 2. Popular culture—United States—
History. 3. Public relations and politics. 4. Celebrities—United States—History. 5. Public
opinion—United States—History. I. Title.
E176.1.S924   1993
973'.099—dc20
                                                          93-33901

Blast Books gratefully acknowledges the generous help of
Beth Escott, Don Kennison, Scott Lindgren, and Chris Potash.

Photography Credits

Pages 5, 11, 14, and 91: Scott Lindgren. / Page 12 courtesy of Doug Kirby, Ken Smith, and Mike Wilkins,
The Roadside America Project. / Pages 17, 21, 23, 24, 26, 27, 29, 30, 33–36, and 38: in the John F.
Kennedy Library. / Page 41: Mike Geissinger, LBJ Library Collection. / Pages 44, 48, 50, 57–59, and 61:
Yoichi R. Okamoto, LBJ Library Collection. / Page 47: Robert Knudsen, LBJ Library Collection. / Pages 49
and 53: Cecil Stoughton, LBJ Library Collection. / Page 54: Kevin Smith, LBJ Library Collection. / Pages
160, 161, and 173: Michael Evans, The White House. / Page 163: Terry Arthur, The White House.
All presidential photographs and documents are from the National Archives and Records Administration.

Published by Blast Books, Inc.
P. O. Box 51
Cooper Station
New York, NY 10276-0051

Designed by Laura Lindgren

Manufactured in the United States of America
First Edition 1993

10 9 8 7 6 5 4 3 2 1

CONTENTS

ACKNOWLEDGMENTS

The National Archives and Records Administration archivists and their assistants at the presidential libraries and the Nixon archives in D.C. were extremely helpful, knowledgeable and friendly. Thanks: Steve Branch, Ken Hafeli, Dave Stanhope, Alan Goodrich, Philip Scott, Richard McNeil, Leesa Tobin, Richard King, Suzanne Barchus, Wendy Sparks and all others.

Russ Smith, publisher and editor of *New York Press,* where I'm happy to work, let me take the time off I needed to make the several research trips. He also let me write a couple of articles that became sections of this book. Thanks, O. Q. Kalea Chapman, who as a research assistant interning at *New York Press* in 1992 made a bunch of trips to the public library for me and found several of the books and articles I cite.

Thanks to Scott Lindgren, who put me up, drove me around and kept me in smokes, food and drink on two research trips to Los Angeles. Hey also to Mr. Nick and Linda and everyone else I've become friends with out there through them.

Special thanks to Ken Swezey, Laura Lindgren, Don Kennison, and Diane Ramo. Oh, and Miz Knucklehed, for not eating it.

THE HUMAN PSEUDO-EVENT

No one governs. Everyone performs.
Joseph Heller

Very early on the morning of December 21, 1970, The King appeared at the northwest gate of the White House and asked to see the president. Anyone else might have been detained by security or at least turned away and told to go through the proper channels. But this wasn't just anyone, this was The King. A few hours later he was in the Oval Office, alone with the president, except for an aide taking notes and an official White House photographer snapping away.

Today, the shot of The King and the president shaking hands is believed to be the best known and most popular photograph ever taken of a president since Lincoln. I was told by a staff person at the Nixon archives in D.C. that it is not only the most requested photo in their holdings but is requested more often than all the thousands upon thousands of other Nixon photos combined. In the gift shop of the Nixon Library & Birthplace in Yorba Linda, southeast of Los Angeles, I scanned the rack of postcards and saw Nixon in China, Nixon with various world leaders, but no Nixon and Elvis. "Oh lord, don't ask," the matronly docent behind the counter sighed. "We can't keep it in stock. It keeps selling out faster than we can order more."

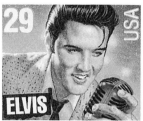
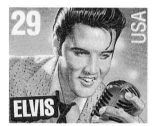

Of course, it is *not* a photo of a president. It's a photo of Elvis Presley *with* a president. *The King and the president.* The most popular man in the world and the most powerful, alone together in the White House, shaking hands. What was it that brought them together?

For Elvis it was famously simple. He wanted a federal drug-enforcement agent's badge to add to his collection of cop paraphernalia. He was told that the only man in the country who could give him a badge was the president. And he must have known that he, Elvis Presley, was about the only man in the country who could simply knock at the White House gate and actually be handed one.

As for Nixon, he later said that he'd scarcely known whom he was shaking hands with that day, beyond his vague awareness that his daughters liked a couple of Elvis' records. It's hard to tell whether this is sincere or just something Nixon said because he thought it fit his image. Either way, it's a statement as bizarre as any of the revelations on his infamous White House tapes. Certainly it suggests a president at least as far out of touch with reality as Elvis was.

Fifteen years after Elvis' death, in 1993 on his birthdate of January 8, the Elvis memorial postage stamp went on sale and drew enormous crowds to post offices around the country. Millions of copies of that stamp were sold in that single day. January 9, 1993, the day after the Elvis stamp went on sale, happened to be Nixon's eightieth birthday. History and mythology sometimes work that way. A January 10 Sunday *New York Times* article reporting on it carried the headline NIXON IS 80 (AND ELVIS JOINS PARTY). The Nixons spent the day in their New Jersey townhouse across the river from Manhattan, while the staff at the Nixon Library & Birthplace, Nixon's shrine to himself—his own Graceland, as it were—threw a symbolic birthday party. "Hundreds of visitors at the Nixon Library posed with life-size photo cutouts of Presley and the former President," the *Times* article reported. "They ooohed and ahhhed as they filed past a display of the wood-handled revolver and the silver bullets that the King gave the President in 1970. . . ."

It went on:

They couldn't help falling in love, but it was hard to tell with whom, Elvis or Mr. Nixon. "Who's Nixon?" asked 40-year-old Shirley Bowman of Lake Forest,

Calif., who bought a $45 watch with a picture of Mr. Nixon and Presley on its face. . . .

"In my lifetime, I believed President Nixon was the best President we ever had," said Gina Scroggins, a housewife from Austin, Calif. But she added: "There's no one like Elvis."

Although ex-president Nixon was not mentioned again in that issue of the *Times,* Elvis' name was invoked in several articles about Bill Clinton's upcoming term and the promise of a pop-culture presidency. Clinton had turned around his foundering traditional campaign focusing on traditional issues (moral, personal, political) by becoming the sax-playing, King-singing, Hollywood-and-MTV-endorsed candidate. His inauguration ceremonies were the most celebrity packed in history. In the early months of his presidency, he earned as much press for his pop-star shmoozing as for his policy endeavors.

Despite the coy surface of these news articles—the sarcasm of the Nixon piece, something approaching astonishment in the Clinton articles—the unspoken message is clear: Elvis is a symbolic link between the two. After a quarter of a century, the real surprise was not that the ghost of Elvis had returned to the White House, but only that it had taken so long.

In *The Image,* first published in 1962, historian Daniel J. Boorstin formulated what was to become a standard line of political analysis over the next few decades: he warned that the mass media, especially television, were ruining American democracy. He articulated two ideas that became universal. One was his coinage, the *pseudo-event,* his term for news created solely for the purpose of having news to report: the pointless press conference, the scripted interview, the photo opportunity. The second was his definition of a celebrity as *a person who is known for his well-knownness.* "He is," Boorstin dolefully remarked, "the human pseudo-event."

The pseudo-event and the celebrity were the creations, Boorstin believed, of modern media, beginning with the proliferation of mass-circulation newspapers and magazines in the mid-1800s and accelerated by tv from the 1950s on. The vast increase in the volume of media created a voracious appetite for news items to fill the pages of newspapers and America's millions of tv screens. If there was no newsworthy event to report, then pseudo-news had to be created; if there were no great men to write about, tout a celebrity. If no news, send rumors.

Boorstin distinguished empty celebrityhood from old-fashioned fame and reputation. "Of course," he conceded, "there never was a time when 'fame' was precisely the same thing as 'greatness.' But, until very recently, famous men and great men were pretty nearly the same group. . . . A man's name was not apt to become a household word unless he exemplified greatness in some way or other. . . . To become known to a whole people a man usually had to be something of a hero: as the dictionary tells us, a man 'admired for his courage, nobility, or exploits.' "

Boorstin was concerned that we had come to admire mere celebrities more than real heroes—The King, say, more than a president. But what really worried him was that we didn't even recognize the distinction anymore, because it had been functionally obliterated:

> We seem to have discovered the processes by which fame is manufactured. . . . Discovering that we . . . can so quickly and so effectively give a man "fame," we have willingly been misled into believing that fame—well-knownness—is still a hallmark of greatness. Our power to fill our minds with more and more "big names" has increased our demand for Big Names and our willingness to confuse the Big Name with the Big Man. . . . We have filled our world with artificial fame. . . .
>
> We can fabricate fame, we can at will . . . make a man or woman well known; but we cannot make him great. We can make a celebrity, but we can never make a hero.

It's no coincidence that Boorstin was writing this in the heart of Kennedy's Camelot. Although he barely mentions Kennedy directly, the general implication was unmistakable. When *The Image* first appeared, Boorstin managed to be out of the country. No wonder, snapped the *New York Times*, insinuating that his opinions were just short of treasonous.

What little *The Image* does say about Kennedy is reported with scathing disdain. Boorstin was one of the first to identify the "Great Debates" between Kennedy and Nixon in 1960, the first televised debates between presidential candidates, as the beginning of the end, "a new kind of political quiz-show . . . remarkably successful in reducing great national issues to trivial dimensions." It was, he wrote, "a clinical example of the pseudo-event, of how it is made, why it appeals, and of its consequences for democracy in America." The performance of either candidate "had only the most dubious relevance—if any at all—to his real qualifications. . . . The great presidents in our history (with the possible exception of F.D.R.) would have done miserably; but our most notorious demagogues would have shone. . . . Finally the television-watching voter was left to judge, not on issues explored by thoughtful men, but on the relative capacity of the two candidates to perform under television stress."

In milder tones, reporter-historian Theodore H. White made basically the same argument in his best-selling *The Making of the President 1960,* published a year earlier than Boorstin's book. White's detailed account of how and why Nixon had made such a disastrous impression on tv was already becoming the most often cited passage in that large book. Though White's analysis did not carry the curmudgeonly tone of Boorstin's, White was deeply troubled by tv's potential to supplant issues with images and he felt that Nixon deserved the "utmost sympathy" for the way tv had robbed him of a fair chance.

The trivialization of American politics, with special attention to television's presumed role in it, has been a favorite topic of analysis ever since. Scores of books and probably thousands of print articles and tv commentaries have addressed the issue—and nearly all have accepted what we might call the Boorstin-White premise as a kind of fundamental belief. Television is bad for politics. It reduces politicians to blow-dried hairdos and distills complex issues into sound bites. It goads gullible voters into making knee-jerk decisions.

Yet political leaders felt it necessary to court the masses throughout history. The fact is, American politicians have long been elected as much on the basis of their popular image—what Boorstin calls celebrity—as on sober analysis of their statesmanship or policies. In an electoral democracy, mass popularity *is* political power.

Two books that brilliantly document this are Leo Braudy's *The Frenzy of Renown,* an encyclopedic history of fame and power since ancient times, and Ronald Brownstein's *The Power and The Glitter,* which focuses specifically on the ongoing love affair between Washington and Hollywood in this century.

Braudy writes that Alexander the Great consciously modeled his public image on the great heroes of Homer, especially Hercules. He "illustrates that the monarchial personality is always a premeditated construction.... Many of the stories about Alexander indicate his special talent for transforming himself into the stuff of symbol and myth." After his death, Ptolemy I issued coins showing Alexander crowned like Hercules with the mane of the Nemean lion, "among the first coins to depict realistically an actual human being." In a sense they are the ancient ancestors of the photographs in this book.

The commissioning of official court portraits, also lineal ancestors to official White House photography today, began during the politically turbulent Renaissance. Lorenzo di Medici, Henry VIII, Elizabeth I and others disseminated their images as popular symbols of their legitimate rule over insecure thrones.

Following in fine tradition, LBJ was commemorated on a plate.

The 1760s, Braudy writes, were "the seedtime of modern visual celebrity. The engraving and printing trade was expanding enormously, and a major part of their output was the reproduction of portraits" of great men like Rousseau, Hume, Voltaire and Ben Franklin. In 1774 "Josiah Wedgwood inaugurated his portrait-medallions of 'illustrious moderns' to bring their images into less prosperous homes." Plates, figurines, pitchers and the like all bore their images. Ben Franklin "by the early 1760s ... was recognizable enough to appear in caricatures without his name being appended." In France, by 1779 a painting of him "done by the official painter to the king of France, is merely labeled 'Vir' (Man)."

The revolutionary founders of the United States understood and exploited their own public images. Braudy explains that "Washington, fully convinced of his own destiny, swiftly became a national symbol ... a unifying image to which all parties could appeal...." A 1776 portrait of Washington by Charles Wilson Peale was "quickly reproduced and sold as an engraving." When Washington died, an entire industry sprang up to feed the hunger for memorial images of him, in Europe as well as America. Often depicted as a Greek or Roman god, he was reproduced in porcelain and Wedgwood, needlepoint and engraving.

At the same time, as Braudy reports, the letters and statements "of virtually any one of the Founding Fathers" are filled with attacks on one another "for their ambition, their greed for praise, their vanity, and so on." For example, Braudy cites a series of letters John Adams wrote to his friend Benjamin Rush between 1805 and 1813, in which Adams

> attacks Washington's immoderate desire for praise and even more the almost "idolatrous" celebrations of Washington once he died. . . . Even when Washington gave a speech, says Adams, he was like Garrick playing Shakespeare: It was all theater. Not that theater doesn't have its political point. The Declaration of Independence, he says, was an effective piece of theater. In fact, says Adams, the creators of the Revolution had purposefully decided to make Washington a symbol of national unity to rival any king; therefore they repressed any negative remarks about his military or political stewardship. Echoing Bolingbroke on Louis XIV, Adams concludes Washington may not have been the greatest president, but he was certainly "the best actor of presidency we have ever had."

In 1849 Matthew Brady took the first photo portrait of a sitting president, James Polk. And Abraham Lincoln became one of Brady's most faithful—and grateful—customers. He said that he owed his election to a "carte de visite" (an early form of the photographic postcard) Brady had made of him, which his supporters distributed widely during his campaign. "I am coming to believe," one of his campaign advisors commented, "that likenesses broadcast are excellent means of electioneering."

The day after Lincoln arrived in Washington he went to Brady's studio there for a new portrait. Between 1847 and his death in 1865, Lincoln is thought to have posed for around 100 photographs—nothing by later standards, but an astounding number for his day. In *Picture Perfect*, media and political analyst Kiku Adatto notes that Lincoln wasn't the only politician exploiting his image at the time. In New York the corrupt Boss Tweed had Brady take a photo that made him look "the picture of probity." Meanwhile, newspaper cartoonists like Thomas Nast were drawing caricatures that came much closer to revealing the crook he really was. "Stop those damn pictures," Tweed is said to have demanded of his b'hoys when he saw Nast's work. "I don't care so much what the papers write about me. My constituents can't read. But damn it, they can see pictures."

Political figures and popular celebrities were also learning how to exploit one another for mutual publicity. Lincoln once interrupted a wartime cabinet meeting to greet the newly wed General and Mrs. Tom Thumb, P. T. Barnum's immensely popular midgets. "The usual explanation is that Lincoln was looking for comic relief in the midst of the awful pressures of the Civil War," Braudy writes. "But he was also entertaining American celebrities whose faces and names were beginning to become at least as recognizable as his own."

Brownstein takes up the story as it accelerates in this century. Teddy Roosevelt, he reports, was one of the most egregious and shameless image-mongers of all presidents. Like FDR and JFK after him, he was a physical weakling who created a macho image by using staged photographs and a charmed press to exaggerate his physical prowess and his exploits as a hunter and fighter.

In February 1915, Brownstein writes,

General and Mrs. Tom Thumb, posed with an anonymous baby.

> The Birth of a Nation *was screened at the White House—apparently the first film shown there. President Woodrow Wilson agreed to see the movie at the request of an old college chum, author Thomas Dixon, Jr., who had written the novel* (The Clansman) *on which [D. W. Griffith's] classic was based. Dixon thought presidential approval might help the film fend off the attacks it instantly faced from black organizations outraged by its positive portrayal of the Ku Klux Klan.*

Wilson responded with a press agent's dream of an endorsement—he called it "like writing history with lightning"—but when the film drew outraged responses anyway, White House spin doctors rushed to deny he'd ever said it.

Al Jolson organized Broadway stars for the Republican presidential campaigns in 1920 and 1924, singing theme songs for Warren Harding ("Harding, You're the Man for

Us") and Calvin Coolidge ("Keep Cool with Coolidge"). In 1929 Herbert Hoover's very first dinner guests at the White House were Louis B. Mayer and his wife. The previous year, Mayer had campaigned furiously to get Hoover elected, mobilizing movie and media types, including Claudette Colbert, Cecil B. DeMille, D. W. Griffith, Walter Huston and, most importantly, newspaper czar William Randolph Hearst. Al Smith, Hoover's Democratic rival, hadn't been wanting for star power either; his came from back home on Broadway—George M. Cohan, Irving Berlin, Helen Hayes, George Gershwin, Georgie Jessel, Eddie Cantor. Mayer threw himself just as furiously into Hoover's doomed reelection campaign in 1932.

Mayer's motivation? On one level, like all businessmen who shmooze with politicians, he was looking for the competitive edge that friends in high places can provide. On a deeper level Mayer, a poor immigrant Jew, a failed junk dealer turned movie mogul and millionaire, was combating his desperate fear of appearing uncultured, unimportant and, especially, un-American. He yearned for acceptance by those he perceived as the country's true power brokers and elite.

And Hoover's motivation? Brownstein writes:

For politicians, associating with celebrities is, consciously or not, part of a search for legitimacy at the most fundamental level.

Establishing such legitimacy is arguably the most delicate task politicians in democratic societies face. In monarchies, the legitimacy of government derives from Heaven or tradition; in dictatorships, power makes the very question moot. But in democratic societies the social basis of governmental authority is constantly shifting and must be constantly reaffirmed. Democratic leaders are never free of the need to legitimize their rule by grounding themselves in the traditions of their nation.

By the mid-1930s, the selling of political candidates through celebrity endorsements on radio was commonplace. Sober political analysts complained of radio's pernicious influence in gloomy terms very much like later pronouncements against tv.

Ronald Reagan may have been the first president who had been an actor, but Franklin Delano Roosevelt was the first to have been a failed screenwriter. In 1920, after Warren Harding defeated the Democratic ticket of James M. Cox and FDR, the young Roosevelt went into the law and surety bonds business in New York City and set to work on a short screenplay based on the life of his hero John Paul Jones. Roosevelt being a well-known political figure, the completed screenplay was politely received, and then quietly shelved, by the New York agency Famous Players–Lasky Corporation.

Arthur Krock called FDR "the best showman the White House has ever lodged." Roosevelt's dinner table was often adorned with celebrity guests like Melvyn and Helen Gahagan Douglas, Douglas Fairbanks, and moguls Darryl F. Zanuck and Jack Warner. FDR's radio campaigns in 1940 and 1944 featured Humphrey Bogart, Henry Fonda, Groucho Marx, Judy Garland, James Cagney and Edward G. Robinson. The Democrats' "most glittering recruit" in '44 was "the nation's newest pop superstar: Frank Sinatra." Bobbysocksers wore lapel buttons proclaiming FRANKIE'S FOR F.D.R. AND SO ARE WE.

For all that, Brownstein says, "Roosevelt showed no signs of being dazzled by Hollywood glamour.... Roosevelt seemed to sense how keenly the moguls craved the social validation of a White House dinner or an autographed photo of the president on their desk—proof that they stood in the company of powerful and serious men, even if they were not allowed into Los Angeles' country clubs."

Roosevelt was also an exceptional master of publicity and press, and the extraordinary lengths to which he would go to control his image became a model subsequently emulated by later presidents. In *The Mortal Presidency*, political scientist Robert Gilbert describes the remarkable stage-management that kept FDR's polio-crippled legs a secret for most of his uniquely long presidency. The deception was well under way by the time FDR first ran for the presidency: ". . . Roosevelt's aides made every effort to portray the Democratic nominee as a man who had conquered polio and who could walk. As he traveled across the country, his leg braces, without which he could not stand, had to be put on and locked into place before each campaign appearance. . . . The lecterns at which he spoke were normally bolted to the floor so that he could lean on them for support. . . ."

At the White House, "no pictures of Roosevelt in his wheelchair were permitted. . . . If this rule was violated, members of the Secret Service were not averse to seizing the camera of the offending party and exposing the film. Photographs were normally taken from the waist up, and those that did show FDR's leg braces were generally touched up so as to be obscured."

After FDR, the romance between Hollywood and Washington went sour for a time. For years Hollywood intellectual circles had been dominated by leftists and liberals, and Washington was in a panic of red-baiting; they collided in the House Un-American Activities Committee hearings and blacklisting. When Eisenhower ran in 1952, Hollywood was desperate to shed its pinko image and went all out for Ike. Producers and directors stage-managed his appearances and the Republican convention. Brownstein recounts that actor Robert Montgomery "advised Eisenhower on his gestures, the use of makeup, relaxing for the [television] camera." After the election he often visited the White House as the president's "personal television consultant" and helped to orchestrate the 1956 Republican convention. ". . . In those early years of the television age," Brownstein writes, "a president receiving dramatic advice from an actor conjured up images of the ventriloquist's dummy."

After Adlai Stevenson lost the 1952 presidential race—the first one in which television began to play a significant role—one of his aides presciently carped, sooner or later "presidential campaigns will have professional actors as candidates who can speak the lines."

Though he didn't invent celebrity politics, in 1960 JFK took it to a whole new level. He enjoyed an extraordinary confluence of money, privilege, looks, youth, sex appeal, the backing of both Hollywood and the news media, and the coming of age of tv. Early Hollywood, searching for the words to describe the exceptional charisma of the true stars, could only come up with *It.* And among the Kennedys, it was agreed that JFK had *It.* More than any president since Teddy Roosevelt, he was a celebrity himself, President Heart Throb, the first pop-star president. He was to politics what Elvis was to rock and roll, what Marilyn was to Hollywood starlets.

Like all great pop stars, he benefited from the luck of perfect timing. He appeared as representative of a new generation in American politics at a time when that was exactly

JOHN F. KENNEDY
1917 — 1963

what people desired. Writing on the very cusp of Kennedy's triumph in the fall of 1960, Norman Mailer tried to explain it this way:

Since the First World War Americans have been leading a double life, and our history has moved on two rivers, one visible, the other underground; there has been the history of politics which is concrete, factual, practical and unbelievably dull . . . and there is a subterranean river of untapped, ferocious, lonely and romantic desires, that concentration of ecstasy and violence which is the dream life of the nation. . . . When the West was filled, the expansion turned inward, became part of an agitated, overexcited, superheated dream life. . . . [In Hollywood] the romantic possibilities of the old conquest of land turned into a vertical myth, trapped within the skull, of a new kind of heroic life, each choosing his own archetype . . . be it Barrymore, Cagney, Flynn, Bogart, Brando or Sinatra.

The Eisenhower fifties, Mailer felt, had stifled America's wild side; even our movies had become bland and conformist. "The life of politics and the life of myth had diverged too far." If Kennedy hadn't come along to reunite the two, our yearnings would have created some other figure very like him.

However arguable his policy accomplishments, it's unarguable that Kennedy changed the face of American politics—if only the face of it. He set a mark of celebrity that almost every politician since, from presidential hopefuls to candidates for city sewer commissioner, must contend with. Having looked so bad beside Kennedy in 1960, Nixon had Madison Avenue build an entirely new image and ad campaign for him in 1968. Ford surrounded himself with celebrities in the vain hope that a little glitter would rub off on his lusterless image. Jimmy Carter utterly failed to control his image and was crushed by an opponent who consisted of almost nothing but image.

Combining Kennedy's glamour and good timing with Nixon's Madison Avenue publicity techniques (and staff), Ronald Reagan was the very image of "image politics." He serves as the end-point of an historical arc that begins with JFK, from the president as celebrity to the celebrity as president.

Though it reached an apex in Reagan's administration, image politics hardly ended there. George Bush used pop stars and movie stars and waged video game wars to distract voters and the press from his own colorless image. Bill Clinton marshaled more celebrities and pop culture iconography than any candidate in history, even reaching out to The King for help.

In the course of writing this book, I traveled to all the relevant presidential libraries, beginning with an exploratory trip to the Nixon archives in D.C. They're all different from one another in ways that reflect the presidents to whom they're dedicated. North of Los Angeles, Ronald Reagan's library is a kind of Stretch Mission affair, a Hollywood fantasy hacienda of red tile roofs and shaded courtyards on a ponderosa scale. It sits on the naked knob of a hill with an authoritative view of the entire Simi Valley, a very white, very Republican suburban kraal.

LBJ's and JFK's libraries are lofty, heroic exercises in modernist design. LBJ's is a huge white cube of a mausoleum very near the campus of the University of Texas in Austin. JFK's, designed by I. M. Pei, is a boldly triangular expanse of glass evoking a sailboat with a favorable breeze; it's at water's edge south of Boston's harbor. Carter's facility, in Atlanta, characteristically eschews bombast; a donut of red brick, it is sunk so low in tasteful, naturalistic landscaping that it almost disappears. The Gerald R. Ford Library, the humblest of all, also suits his image perfectly. On the campus of the University of Michigan in Ann Arbor, it's a plain, totally unprepossessing red brick box. It looks like Gerald Ford Junior High School.

The Nixon Library & Birthplace in Yorba Linda is an anomaly. Nixon resigned in disgrace in August of 1974. One month later, when Gerald Ford granted him a blanket pardon for any involvement in Watergate, he also sealed a deal with Nixon for "shared custody" of his White House documents, to be archived in a facility in California. The largely Democratic Congress, fearing that Nixon might destroy Watergate-related materials, quickly passed legislation "mandating that all the documents of the Nixon Administration—perhaps 42 million pages, and some 4,000 hours of tape recordings, on 950

Richard Nixon's birthplace.

reels—be taken out of his hands" and looked after by the National Archives and Records Administration (NARA) in a Washington facility (Seymour Hersh, *The New Yorker,* December 14, 1992).

As of 1993 the NARA is still looking after those documents in what amounts to a U-Stor-It warehouse just outside the D.C. Beltway. Nixon's California Library & Birthplace is an imposing marble-and-granite structure that dominates a sweeping lawn, with an impressive glass arc at its entry that evokes the semicircular portico of the White House. Inside is a lavish museum dedicated to Nixon's career and exploits.

In 1993 his wife was buried there. This Taj Mahalesque shrine is a whited sepulchre. The actual library at the Nixon Library is effectively hidden in the basement, out of public view. When I visited in the fall of 1991, it was absolutely clean of presidential records. Not a single volume on the shelves, not a sheet of White House notepaper in the files. The only use it saw was as a space occasionally rented for formal dinners and Hollywood "wrap" parties. Situated nearby is a tiny white cottage you might at first mistake for the groundskeeper's home, but which is, in fact, the house where Nixon was born, preserved as a tiny museum annex.

Presidential libraries are not lending libraries. They are run by NARA, and the NARA archivists aren't librarians, but historians or political scientists. Those you meet at a particular library aren't necessarily experts in or admirers of that president. They tend to be federal civil servants who simply got posted there. However, the director of each museum usually is a crony whose appointment was personally approved by that president, and sometimes there are former White House staffers or other cronies mixed into the library's administration.

Beyond simply cataloging a library's documents—in itself an exhaustive, years-long process—the archivists review it all in light of the 1978 Presidential Records Act to determine what can be opened to public view and what's to be restricted for reasons of national security or personal privacy. By law, the ex-presidents themselves have a lot of control over when and how much of the private documents are open to public view. Presidents Ford and Carter are very open about this, while the Kennedy family guards his private documents quite jealously, and Nixon has, as of 1993, kept the bulk of his records hidden behind a thicket of legal disputes.

When I visited the Reagan Library in 1993, two years after its official opening, the archivists had made about 6.5 million of 47 million pages available to the public, all covering low-priority activities of his administration about which they could make quick and easy rulings under the '78 law: agriculture, civil aviation, sports, public relations, highways and bridges, that sort of thing. There are national security records that archivists won't even review for thirty years. When I asked a pair of archivists how long it will be before the whole Reagan collection is reviewed, they both laughed ruefully. "We'll be dead," one of them said.

The White House photographs are among the first documents to be opened for public view. But even some photos are restricted for reasons of personal privacy. At the Reagan Library, for example, photos of Nancy Reagan with Frank Sinatra had been pulled from the public collection, no doubt in response to gossip writer Kitty Kelley's suggestion that the two had conducted an affair in the White House.

For the most part, however, any citizen who wants to do research in a presidential library is free to pore over thousands upon thousands of photographs, usually printed as contact sheets and stored in three-ring binders. Because these are government documents, there are no copyright restrictions on their use. As citizens, we all share in their ownership. You simply pay the reproduction cost—anywhere from $5 to $15 per photo in 1993—and NARA mails you the prints. You're free to do what you like with them . . . for instance, reproduce them in a book.

If the successful are America's aristocracy, then successful celebrities, whether they're pop stars or presidents, are the figures of our popular mythology. It's a democratic and peculiarly American mythology, kind of tacky, kind of do-it-yourself—and for those very qualities, very seductive and appealing. Not just to the celebrities themselves, not just to Americans, but globally.

"Don't take myth lightly," semiotician Marshall Blonsky warns in *American Mythologies:*

Behind it is the enormous power of modern industrial production coupled with a formidable myth-generating communication industry that is bringing about a new, planetary culture system. . . . The collapse of the Wall, the crisis in the formerly socialist world, and the failure of Third World wars are rooted not only in economic and political reality, but in a mythological impotence, and inability to produce personally felt icons and objects. Next to Barbie and Batman, Madonna and EuroDisney, there seems to be nothing comparable in the culture of the peripheral regions. . . .

The socialist myths were purely political and short-lived. The hammer and the sickle, Lenin and Che were myths of struggle and war, not of pleasure and play. Not even Yuri Gargarin, the Soviet cosmonaut, had the right stuff. Although many might question the value and depth of contemporary western myths, like it or not, they have shown their world appeal and tenacity in spite of the mystery of their surface and their plastic, nonbiodegradable power; their smoke-and-mirror nature. It's not an Orwellian nightmare or a Renaissance ideal, but we must recognize their promiscuity and, for a moment, withhold judgment, the better to analyze the phenomenon.

JFK- MART

Camelot was fun, even for the peasants,
as long as it was televised to their huts.
Joe McGinnis

Late in December 1991, an auction drew a crowd to a banquet room in New York City's Omni Park Central hotel. It was not a standard turnout for an auction. Half the crowd was newspeople, with all the customary lights and cameras and boom mics, shoving and elbowing, newspaper reporters scribbling in notepads, tv reporters gingerly patting their hairdos. Only a handful of the others in the room were actually there to bid, and the rest were there to gawk.

The grim epicenter of all the commotion was Earl Ruby, brother of Jack Ruby and executor of his estate, looking very much the small, elderly, retired dry cleaner from Michigan he was. He handled the media with a sometimes peckish gruffness. "I'm sweatin'," he muttered glumly under the glaring tv lights.

No, Earl told reporters, his brother was not part of any assassination conspiracy. He wasn't a hired Mafia hit man. He just saw Lee Harvey Oswald swaggering down the hall with that Lee Harvey Oswald smirk on his face and went into a spasm of righteous indignation. Though it was a gut shot at point blank range, Earl insisted that his brother wasn't trying to kill Oswald. He just wanted to "punish" him.

Earl bristled when a reporter asked him about the morality of profiting from the Kennedy tragedy. "Profit?" he barked. "How the hell am I gonna profit?" He insisted

Page 17. *Kennedy with singer Julie London.*

that his brother's back taxes and legal fees would eat up whatever came in from the auction.

Newspaper photographers shoved and shouted at one another to get out of the way. They complained that the tv cameras were getting special treatment. One of them prowled the edge of the crowd singing, "Oh Rooooby, don't take your love to town."

There were 335 lots in the auction. First came autographs of celebrities: John Glenn, P. T. Barnum, Babe Ruth, Clint Eastwood, Chairman Mao, Boris Yeltsin, Salvador Dali, Bob Dylan. Bugsy Siegel's passport was on the block. Bing Crosby's signature went for $400. So did John Quincy Adams'. The signatures of the Three Stooges went for a mere $150.

Then came the items everyone had come to gawk at. A 1949 signed letter from JFK. A Jim Garrison signature went for $475. So did a signed letter from Dr. Robert Shaw of the medical team who first examined JFK's bullet-ridden body in Dallas. A Jack Ruby guest card to the Dallas Club Latino brought in $350.

Finally, the star lot: Jack Ruby's .38 Colt. The auctioneer held it up for the cameras. The crowd surged forward. Someone knocked the auctioneer's microphone from his podium. The bidding started at $100,000 and ended at $200,000. The winner would later be revealed as the agent of an anonymous New Jersey gun collector. As soon as the bidding was over, he ran out a back door, with the entire crowd of newspeople literally on his heels.

Suddenly Earl Ruby's mood had brightened. Standing over in a corner, he was grinning from ear to ear. He couldn't stop mentioning that Jack had bought the gun for $62.50. . . .

It wasn't a great moment in JFK lore, just a typical one that bore several familiar earmarks: the media circus, the morbid gawking, the shimmer of violence. The haphazard, vulgar jumble of big men and big names, statesmen and stooges distinguished only by their price tags. Remnants of history reduced for quick sale. Camelot after the peasants have taken over. We paid our respects for several years. And then, with the rudeness that is public curiosity, we invaded the shrine, undressed his corpse, touched his wounds and came away doubting—yet obsessed. If it's not the way Kennedy or the Kennedys would want him to be remembered, what's more important is that he is still remembered, thirty years later, still obsessed about even at this great and shabby remove.

✦   ✦   ✦

JFK entered the White House looking like a glamorous movie star, became a tv star while he was there, and went out as a semidivine hero of popular mythology. Like Reagan, he made it look easy. Like Reagan, he had trained for it all his life.

When he graduated from Choate in 1935, Kennedy's classmates voted him most likely to succeed, despite his mediocre academic record and lack of varsity sports. Maybe they already saw in him the glimmer of what Jackie later called "the shining light" and others might call star quality.

In *The Kennedys* Peter Collier and David Horowitz describe how, as early as

JFK greets a coy-looking Dorothy Provine.

the 1920s, Joseph Kennedy foresaw the way popular celebrity and political power would converge in America and moved on both fronts to prepare the way for his offspring. Much of John Kennedy's casual charisma, his easy grace before cameras, the way he charmed the press and through them, the public, was the fruit of careful preparation. Collier and Horowitz write that he "made his father's credo his own: It is not what a person is that counts, but what people think he is."

For decades Joseph Kennedy carefully husbanded the fields of political power and social prestige for his children, first in Boston, then nationally, then internationally. An Irish Catholic from the wrong end of Boston, he was the consummate social climber. No wonder he understood Hollywood, the glitter palace also built by outsiders, and saw its opportunities. He began with taking over a chain of movie houses and triumphed with the merger that became RKO. He impulsively wooed Hollywood's top names, from the moguls ("that bunch of pants pressers in Hollywood making themselves millionaires") to his mistress Gloria Swanson, whom he brought home to meet the wife and kids. When the kids were sick he had Tom Mix and Gary Cooper write to them.

John Kennedy was a regular visitor in Hollywood from the mid-1930s on. It attracted him the same way it did his dad. He evidently slept with his first starlet during a summer off from school in the mid-thirties and continued to do so over the years, right up to his death—with Gene Tierney, reputedly Marilyn Monroe, Angie Dickinson (who denied it), Jayne Mansfield (who said he was lousy), maybe Grace Kelly and scores or possibly hundreds of lesser starlets and chorus girls.

According to anecdote, when Kennedy, by then a senator, was in the hospital slowly recuperating from radical spinal surgery, Jackie got Grace Kelly to dress up in nurse's whites and snuck her into his room. Kennedy was in such pain he barely seemed interested. "I must be losing it," Kelly sighed.

The strange image of Jackie pimping starlets for her husband (if only by gesture) is mind boggling, but also curious is Kennedy's limp reaction. As was true for his father, sex seems to have been more a delicious perk of Hollywood than its real appeal; Collier and Horowitz report that young JFK was "fascinated not only by the tinsel and glitter but by the way that sex appeal, even more than sex itself, became power; by the way ordinary people came to inhabit the extraordinary celluloid identities created for them. . . ."

A friend from that time tells Collier and Horowitz: "Charisma wasn't a catchword yet, but Jack was very interested in that binding magnetism these screen personalities had. What exactly was *it*? How did you go about acquiring it? Did it have an impact on your private life? How did you make it work for you? He couldn't let the subject go."

By the mid-fifties, as Kennedy set his sights on the White House, he had Hollywood in his back pocket. Especially that element in Hollywood that would identify itself as young, hip, swinging and liberal. Since the postwar years Hollywood liberals had taken a beating from conservative Washington—the House Un-American Activities Committee trials, blacklisting and then the long, dull fifties, when the studios forced them to make safe, conformist family entertainment. Kennedy represented a whole new generation of politics, a whole new *style*—young, hip, swinging and liberal. After many years of mutual

Jackie—admired here by Prince Rainier—once pimped Grace to a curiously limp Jack.

hobnobbing and partying, they felt that he was one of them. Peter Lawford was part of the family. Kennedy and Marlon Brando could kid each other about their weight. He offered Kirk Douglas advice on which roles to take. Steve Allen summed it up best when he said that Kennedy and his clan were "kind of hip and easy to talk to. They just seemed like one of the gang."

By the time the 1960 Democratic convention was held, appropriately in Los Angeles, even literary heavyweights like Norman Mailer were unable to rise above movie star clichés when trying to describe the excitement Kennedy, or at least what he represented, was generating. Covering the convention for *Esquire*, Mailer described the moment of Kennedy's triumphant arrival to accept his nomination for president:

> For one moment he saluted Pershing Square, and Pershing Square saluted him back, the prince and the beggars of glamour staring at one another across a city street, one of those very special moments in the underground history of the world ... and one had a moment of clarity, intense as a déjà vu, for the scene which had taken place had been glimpsed before in a dozen musical comedies; it was the scene where the hero, the matinee idol, the movie star comes to the palace to claim the princess. . . . Finally it was simple: the Democrats were going to nominate a man who, no matter how serious his political dedication might be, was indisputably and willy-nilly going to be seen as a great box-office actor, and the consequences of that were staggering and not at all easy to calculate.

Kennedy, Mailer wrote, "would be the most conventionally attractive young man ever to sit in the White House ... America's politics would now be also America's favorite movie, America's first soap opera, America's best-seller. . . ."

It's a sign of how easily the Kennedys merged politics and Hollywood that during the convention John Kennedy stayed in the apartment of comedian Jack Haley, while his father stayed in Marion Davies' house. (Meanwhile, Theodore White reports, convention delegates flocked to Disneyland, which "outdrew all the night clubs of Los Angeles combined.")

Ann-Margret shimmies like a houri at JFK's 1963 birthday bash.

*Once Jackie ruled in Maison
Blanche, less glamorous
New York talents replaced the
Hollywood starlets.*

In *The Power and The Glitter*, Ronald Brownstein writes that "more than any president before or since, Kennedy testified to the irresistible attraction between power and glamour." And of all his Hollywood relationships, that attraction—and its downside—may be most clearly revealed in his honorary membership in the Rat Pack.

The Rat Pack embodied Hollywood's most elemental myth, its deepest unspoken appeal—that as its final reward, fame offered a life without the constraints of fidelity, monogamy, sobriety, and the dreary obligation to show up at a job every morning. . . . In the popular imagination, Sinatra and Kennedy symbolized the union of politics and show business, as if the two men were ambassadors for distinct branches in the American aristocracy of fame. . . . In the long history of Hollywood's relationship with politics, this was probably the pivotal moment. A bond that could not be broken was forged. . . . It hinted at the existence of a society where anyone who was famous mingled with everyone else who was famous, where all lines converged. What politician, what star, wouldn't want to be accepted into that company?

Kennedy looks genuinely relaxed with Jimmy Durante in New York.

Sinatra had met John Kennedy through Lawford—the "Brother-in-Lawford," Sinatra called him—in the mid-fifties. Sinatra "turned up regularly at the strategy sessions Kennedy and his men convened for political leaders at Lawford's oceanfront house as the 1960 campaign approached,"

Brownstein writes. "To all appearances, Kennedy and Sinatra genuinely enjoyed each other's company. . . ." Kennedy "admired the singer's smirking attitude toward life and shared his hostility to stuffy propriety." It was in Las Vegas, where the Rat Pack was filming *Ocean's Eleven,* that Sinatra introduced Kennedy to Judith Campbell (later Exner), who'd had affairs with both Sinatra and mobster Sam Giancana.

Sinatra organized a galaxy of stars to campaign for Kennedy all over the country in 1960. How he must have loved it when a *Boston Globe* writer noted that seeing JFK's effect on women was "like watching a crowd of Frank Sinatra fans." Brownstein writes that Sinatra

wore the relationship with Kennedy, said one friend, "as a man would wear a bou-tonniere." Sinatra sent JFK his albums, fixed up a guest house at his Palm Springs home in anticipation of presidential visits (he even added a heliport), and glowed with pleasure from the most casual interaction. . . . Sinatra treated the relation-ship with uncharacteristic gravity: framing Kennedy's casual notes, even putting a plaque on the door of the room in his home where the candidate had slept. . . .

No one around him doubted that Sinatra believed he had a real friend in the White House. During the convention, Sinatra had reportedly turned to Lawford and said, "We're on our way to the White House, buddy boy. "

Legend has it that during a political function Sinatra was once buttonholed by Sam Rayburn, Speaker of the House and among the very most powerful men in Washington. Sinatra either didn't know or didn't care who Rayburn was, and he wasn't paying him much attention. Exasperated, Rayburn grasped Sinatra's lapel to emphasize a point of conversation. Sinatra stared at him coldly and said, "Take your hands off the suit, creep."

This was around the peak time Sinatra was enjoying his arrogant swagger in the halls of power. By the inauguration, Kennedy was already beginning to pull away from him. Sinatra threw a gala inaugural party at which Kennedy arrived late and didn't stay long. It was the beginning of the end. Jackie didn't like Sinatra. And J. Edgar Hoover was feeding Robert Kennedy the embarrassing truth about Sinatra's and Campbell's mob

JFK matching star quality with the Brother-in-Lawford.

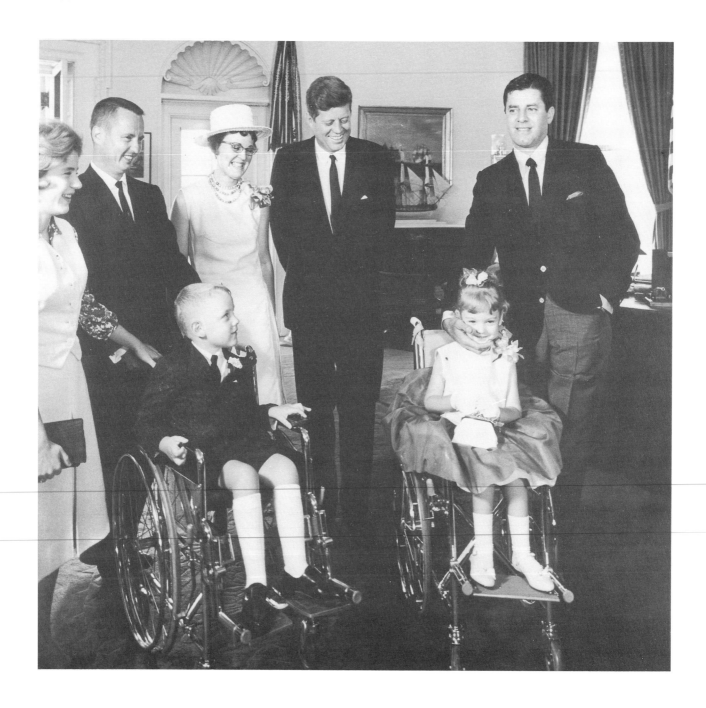

connections. During the first year of the administration Sinatra was invited to a few family weekends at Hyannis Port, and he and the president partied a few more times out West. But little by little his phone calls weren't returned, his gifts were acknowledged with form letters. After entertaining the hope that Sinatra would be a direct line to the Oval Office, the mob decided he was a punk and a braggart.

The final blowup came in the winter of 1962. Kennedy was going to Palm Springs, and Sinatra was fully expecting Kennedy would stay with him. At the recommendation of either the Secret Service or Robert Kennedy, the president stayed at Republican Bing Crosby's instead. In his memoirs, JFK friend and advisor Kenneth O'Donnell recalls that Peter Lawford was "hysterical," and that "later we heard that Sinatra was so incensed that he took a sledge hammer and smashed up the landing pad that he had built for the President's helicopter."

Sinatra later became a Republican and was to have better luck shmoozing Richard Nixon.

In retrospect, the break with Sinatra was to be expected. Kennedy the candidate of a new generation could be an honorary member of the Rat Pack. Kennedy the president of the United States could not. From the instant he walked out of Sinatra's inaugural party, he cultivated a new image, that of a mature world leader. He was of course still glamorous, but in a new way.

From then on it was Jackie, not Frankie, who set the tone of JFK's public image, and the tone was tony. She was a francophilic Bouvier determined to transform "the dreary Maison Blanche," as she called it, into "an oasis of culture" in America. Jack could still have his starlets and parties in private. In public, the president and First Lady partied with the likes of Igor Stravinsky, Maria Callas, John Dos Passos, Aaron Copland, Robert Penn Warren and Gian Carlo Menotti.

As president, JFK rarely appeared in public with mere entertainers. Later presidents, working hard to inject their images with some of that casual Kennedyesque glitz, would be much more avid about photo ops with the stars. When he did let entertainers appear

A visit from Jerry's Kids became an annual event at the White House.

near him, the occasion would be formal and the social lines clearly drawn—a Democratic fundraiser, say, with the stars there to entertain their commander in chief. And they tended to be his old Hollywood cronies less often than figures from the slightly classier Broadway stage, which Jackie preferred. Whenever reminders of the president's wild youth resurfaced in public—Marilyn and Ann-Margret shimmying for him like *houris* at his New York birthday parties in '62 and '63—the new Kennedy was visibly uncomfortable.

It would be years before the public was made aware just how many closed-door parties and how many sexual antics Kennedy had going behind that carefully modulated public image. The complicity of the press in maintaining this secrecy, now so incomprehensible, was another gift from Joseph Kennedy.

JFK had a long and intimate relationship with the press. As Joe Kennedy's kid he'd been surrounded by newsmen and cameras since childhood. He had done a brief stint as a Hearst reporter after the war. When he first ran for Congress, his father's connections ensured him an unprecedented level of national news coverage, from Pathé newsreels in the movie houses to feature profiles in *Time*.

Significantly, Jacqueline also lived much of her life in the news. She had been a regular item in the society pages since her childhood. When she met Jack she was enjoying her own brief newspaper career as the "Inquiring Camera Girl" for the *Washington Times-Herald*; she interviewed him for her page. They'd been introduced at a dinner arranged by Charles Bartlett, the Washington desk of the *Chattanooga Times*. Together, she and Jack made a powerful media team. A close friend said of them, "They were both *actors* and I think they appreciated each other's performances." (It looks ludicrously stiff and kitschy now, but the televised tour she gave of the White House, with her wide and glassy eyes and her breathy Marilyn voice, was one of her most successful performances. To an audience who remembered Mamie Eisenhower and Eleanor Roosevelt, she presented a stunningly crypto-erotic combination of beauty, class, glamour, and *style*.)

"A careful courting of the press played a major part in his rapid rise from a junior senator with a playboy image to a political figure of national consequence," Clarence Wyatt reports in *Paper Soldiers*. Kennedy's publicity staff, directed by the young Pierre Salinger, "raise[d] press relations to the level of art." When Kennedy spoke to reporters, he "informed

Bob Hope and a White House guard compare shnozzes for the prez.

them, he amused them, but most of all he charmed them." Even Henry Luce, ultra-conservative power behind the Time-Life empire and a friend to Richard Nixon, admitted that Kennedy "seduces me.... When I'm with him I feel like a whore."

The press complied in hiding not only his sexual activities but the true extent of Kennedy's physical frailties as well. The public was made aware of his crippling back problems, which were exploited as an integral feature of his heroic image. But, as with FDR and Eisenhower, the often debilitating agony he suffered from his weak back was a closely guarded secret. Only by the rarest chance was he seen on the crutches he was forced to use when his back was under the greatest strain. When speaking in public or on tv, his brisk, short walks to the podium were as carefully staged as FDR's had been.

Above. Dinah Shore bares her pearlies for two buff hunks.

In *The Mortal Presidency*, Robert Gilbert lists other diseases Kennedy suffered at various times in his life. They included malarial fever, diptheria, whooping cough, numerous allergies, hypothyroidism, asthma, severe colitis and Addison's disease, a slow adrenal failure that increased the riskiness of back surgery. To counteract the Addison's he used a hormonal drug in the form of time-released pellets that had to be implanted in his thigh. Supplies of the pellets were kept in safe deposit boxes around the country.

The most persuasive testament to Kennedy's remarkable image control is the way he aikidoed all of the above into a public impression of youthful zest, athleticism and "vigah." The skin discoloration caused by the Addison's was passed off as a healthy tan. The bloat produced by cortisone injections he took to counteract allergies made him look plump and healthy. (At least on tv; in photos, his face appears sometimes almost freakishly bloated and distended in a way that looks decidedly unhealthy.) It's possible that some of his

Opposite. A rare photo of JFK and food. The bloat is from cortisone shots, not over-eating. Billy Graham grins.

famously energetic bounce came from amphetamines injected into his neck to get him over the crippling back agonies.

Kennedy's use of the televised press conference, a format he pioneered and at which he was more effective than any president since him, was brilliant. He had ridden Hollywood and his movie star appeal into power. In the White House he cemented that power by transforming himself into a tv star. Which, as anyone in Hollywood then or now knows, is a very different career. In movies, everything is on a giant scale, fantastical and epochal and far removed from reality. Movies are a tribal, communal ritual. Television is the medium of the living room and bedroom, intimate and chatty. Used well, the tv is a president's direct channel to the voters, bypassing the press, the experts, rival political powers—and the tv powers themselves. All presidents from Kennedy on have known this, but only Kennedy and Reagan have been accomplished enough performers to pull it off.

Chuck Conners, surprisingly, shmoozed several presidents and at least one Soviet premiere.

Like Nixon, Kennedy had recognized the political potential of tv in its early stages. Four years before he ran for the presidency, he was already exploiting tv to prep the nation for his candidacy. Offered the chance to give the nominating speech for Adlai Stevenson at the 1956 Democratic convention, he tore up the text that had been prepared by the party machine and wrote one of his own in ten hours. Before a vast tv audience, he shamelessly exhorted Democrats to "think beyond the balloting of tonight . . . think instead of the four years ahead"—a thinly disguised message to party members and the public at large to look ahead to his future campaign.

Kennedy demonstrated his uncanny understanding of the medium in the 1960 debates. Nixon treated them as just that: debates. His delivery was stiff, formal, declamatory, rhetorical. Kennedy looked calm, tanned, rested, relaxed. He spoke straight into the camera, through the camera, and rather than debating policy with Nixon, he expressed his vision and his goals to the people.

Both Boorstin and White made much of a poll that indicated that people who listened only to the first and crucial debate on the radio felt that Nixon had won. They took it as proof that the visual spectacle of tv—the way it made Nixon look pale and shifty while Kennedy appeared as the handsome personification of grace under pressure—distracted people from the substance of what was being said. Their interpretation has often been quoted as gospel by other writers, even though it completely missed the point. *Kennedy was not debating Nixon.* Kennedy was making a televised appearance before the nation. Nixon was, at best, merely playing second banana, the dowdy old Brand X to Kennedy's New Improved image.

Once he became president, Kennedy seemed to be on tv all the time: trotting athletically to the podium, bantering casually with reporters on a first-name basis, flashing his winningly mischievous wit. He forged an intimate bond of affection with millions of Americans that was almost entirely divorced from anything he actually said or did. Unfortunately for his successors, he set a level of tv competence that the public came to expect but that few could match.

Kennedy didn't bother much with official White House photography. His father had provided him with his own personal photographer, Jacques Lowe, a magazine freelancer by career. During the last five years of Kennedy's life, Lowe shot some forty thousand photos of him, more than all the photos taken by White House photographers during his term.

Kennedy had three photographers assigned to the White House, all of whom were borrowed from other branches of the government: two were military photographers and one was from the Park Service, which was responsible for the White House grounds. They could hardly be called professional portrait photographers, and except for a few lucky breaks, most of their work was barely a notch above amateur snapshots.

*JFK's absence in this photo
is eerily prophetic. Danny Kaye
sits in for him.*

Kennedy severely restricted their access to him; intimate or "candid" shots of Kennedy were Lowe's job. The thirty-five thousand official photographs on deposit in the Kennedy Library—a scant amount compared to the archives compiled by administrations from LBJ on—are almost all formal. At White House ceremonies the official photographers recorded only the staged and staid preliminaries—reception lines, stiff black-tie-and-formal-gown group shots on the White House steps—almost always from too great a distance and an unfortunate angle. Never were they allowed to photograph the dinners themselves. As a young candidate, Kennedy was once mortified to see a newspaper photo of himself devouring a hot dog, and he vowed never again to allow himself to be photographed while eating.

Kennedy also refused to wear a hat, in an era when virtually no adult male would be seen in public without one. He thought he looked bad in hats, and he was mystified by politicians' willingness to wear *silly* hats when visiting fire stations, army bases, Italian bakeries and cowboy states. Singlehandedly, he made all American men feel silly about their hats and killed a fashion habit that they'd been blithely carrying on for generations.

That's what stars do.

To die young and tragically is one way true stars fix their place in the heavens. It becomes almost expected of them. Thirty years after his death and still counting, JFK remains an icon of popular culture and mythology. He is as much a presence as Elvis with his miraculous sightings and myriad impersonators. His association with Marilyn is a source of continuing fascination as well. Like all well-handled relics, his image has grown rather shopworn, his shining light irreparably dulled. Yet there's still a lot of that magical *It* in him, a totemic pop-star power that subsequent presidents have had to try to borrow or bury.

When Jackie told Theodore White that life in the White House had been Camelot, she probably had in mind not Malory's tragic myth but the maudlin Broadway show tunes. Mailer's prince and beggars of glamour saluting each other across a great divide come to mind. We don't have royalty in America. We have show business royalty.

UNCLE CORNPONE

AND HIS LITTLE PORKCHOP

Everyone can see what you appear to be, whereas few have direct experience of what you really are.

Niccoló Machiavelli

In his memoirs of the Johnson White House, top aide Joseph A. Califano, Jr., recalls how LBJ gave his people pep talks. Typically, LBJ began with an anecdote:

In the hill country in the spring, the sun comes up earlier, and the ground gets warmer, and you can see the steam rising and the sap dripping. And in his pen, you can see my prize bull. He's the biggest, best-hung bull in the hill country. In the spring he gets a hankering for those cows, and he starts pawing the ground and getting restless. So I open the pen and he goes down the hill, looking for a cow, with his pecker hanging hard and swinging. Those cows get so Goddamned excited, they get more and more moist to receive him, and their asses just start quivering and then they start quivering all over, every one of them is quivering, as that bull struts into their pasture.

That, the president told his staff, is how he wanted legislators to feel about his next piece of legislation: receptive and quivering with expectation.

Page 41. *LBJ and Gregory Peck sit a spell in a field of black-eyed Susans.*

After Camelot, the Johnson White House seemed like . . . well, like Johnson City: a Texas dogpatch at a dusty crossroads miles between truck stops deep in the heart of Texas, the middle of nowhere. Only by ludicrous exaggeration could it take on the airs of being a city. And fifteen miles deeper into nowhere is the LBJ Ranch, a few acres of hilly cow pasture periodically flooded by the unmighty Pedernales River (locally pronounced *perdnalls*). It's not a true cattle baron's limitless spread. Its vistas are modest, even cramped, by those epic standards. But in LBJ's mind and his personal mythology it expanded into an empire he'd built piece by piece over the years through a combination of birthright and hard work and horse trading—his Texas hill country version of Camelot.

A visit to "Johnson Country," where LBJ grew up and died, a dusty, bumpy landscape Johnson often proclaimed was the center of his entire world view, necessarily includes the excruciatingly uninformative ninety-minute tour of the ranch. It runs past the garage where LBJ's huge white Lincoln and little aqua boat-car are parked, past the field paved with two blocks' worth of concrete that once served as the busy presidential airstrip, past the open-air pens where Johnson came to admire his stud bulls, to the reconstructed four-room dog-trot house where cabinet chiefs and top advisors had had to go outside and around the back to use the bathroom. To see the LBJ brand raised like the flag of a comic opera duchy over every lonely armadillo crossing and two-swing playground in the area is to understand much about that other Johnson Country, the one with forty-nine other states around it, where Johnson played the *patrón* on a global scale, lavishly dispensing largesse on the little people who lived and worked on his land, cannily horse trading with and squinting down the handful of other *patrones* who among them were lords of the rest of the world.

The contrast between JFK and LBJ's presidential personae was striking. Whereas JFK had been suave, sexy, cool, sophisticated, heroic, tragic and, eventually, semidivine, Johnson was loud, crass, vulgar, bullying, crafty and power mad. If in private Kennedy had allowed his irrepressible sexual drive to rule, there was nevertheless something ethereal about his public image. Johnson was an overbearing, unapologetically physical presence. He ruled from the throne of the crapper, with the door wide open, barking orders into the phone and simultaneously conducting press interviews. In 1960 Mailer wrote that Johnson

Johnson, Johnson everywhere. No wonder Nixon looks so edgy as he shares an elevator with him.

"was a political animal, sweated like one." The image of a snorting, shitting, balls-swinging political longhorn became, in effect, a kind of logo representing Johnson's presidency.

The Kennedy clan was acutely aware of the contrast. As early as the 1960 Democratic convention, the Kennedys had infuriated and insulted LBJ by inviting him to take the vice president's spot on the ballot and then, having second thoughts, sending Bobby to suggest that it might be best if he were to refuse it. (A Kennedy staffer told Theodore White, "It was always anticipated . . . that we'd offer Lyndon Johnson the nomination; what we never anticipated was that he'd accept.") LBJ, enraged and hurt, sealed everyone's fate by refusing to refuse.

As vice president he was frozen out of the administration, disinvited to crucial meetings, sent on long trips to ride camels in the East—on a tour of the Taj Mahal he startled guides by cutting loose with a big Texas *ya-hoo* inside the dome—and to act as glorified messenger boy in Southeast Asia. He and Lady Bird were the constant butts of Kennedy family jokes and rudeness; it was Jackie, with her Catholic debutante's radar constantly sweeping for other arrivistes, who dubbed them Uncle Cornpone and his Little Porkchop.

The social gap between Johnson's family and the Kennedys haunted LBJ. Califano recalls:

> *As LBJ saw it, there was a poor kid working around the clock at Southwest Texas State Teachers College in San Marcos and there was a rich kid partying through the ivy halls of Harvard with plenty of time to acquire all the social graces in sophisticated Boston. Lyndon Johnson, who had achieved more in each year of his presidency than most chief executives accomplish in all their White House years, was possessed by an internal class struggle with an icon, and tortured by an envy he could not exorcise.*

So Lyndon Johnson began a competition with Kennedy's mythic legacy that in one way or another has marked every president since, even those who have been politically or personally Kennedy's opposites. On the practical and political level, all the grandiose activity that characterized Johnson's presidency—the Great Society, Civil Rights, the

With Carol Channing after a performance of Hello, Dolly!

The hardest working man in politics meets the hardest working man in show business.

Vietnam War, urban renewal, public housing, the space race, the National Endowment for the Arts—was a conscious and publicly proclaimed effort to complete, extend or outdo what Kennedy had started. LBJ adopted federal programs "the way a child eats rich chocolate-chip cookies," Califano writes. In the end what sank him was the inevitable bloat resulting from his compulsive appetite for achievements that would make his legacy greater than Kennedy's. He wanted it all: the guns and the butter and the chocolate chips.

Johnson was also competitive in calculated image production. LBJ insisted on being sworn in as president aboard Air Force One while it was still on the ground in Dallas—still on Texas soil—with Kennedy's bloodstained widow at his side and Kennedy's (now his) official photographer snapping away. The pictures were instantly disseminated to the world as irrefutable documentation that he had, already, assumed power. Ostensibly it was meant to reassure the nation's allies and to send a message to its enemies. But it must also have been intended to thwart even the hint of mutiny from Bobby Kennedy back in Washington and the Kennedy cronies in the press.

✦   ✦   ✦

It was LBJ who created the first official White House photography office. The result was not only an increase in the number of official images produced but an improvement in photographic quality, since professionals were now employed along with aim-and-shoot military photographers. Whereas JFK had strictly controlled the pictures they were allowed to take, Johnson gave his photographers extraordinarily free access to his private and candid life. They were with him everywhere, all the time, snapping away like public-service *paparazzi*. So ever-present were they that they eventually caused Johnson a minor embarrassment. At a time when he was making a pronounced public show of belt-tightening in his administration's spending—LBJ was known to prowl around the White House at evening time to switch off lights that didn't need to be lit—reporters got hold of the White House's extravagant bill for flashbulbs and teased him about it in print. Johnson appeared to be outraged, and he banished his photographers from the White House grounds for a few days, but it was a rare hiatus for them.

Johnson employed a variety of smaller symbolic gestures he intended would link his administration to the JFK legacy while they quietly seared his own LBJ brand on the new order. For example, he decided to retain the Kennedy name *Honey Fitz* for the presidential yacht, and he had a Kennedyesque rocking chair installed in the Oval Office and often posed for photographs in it (though of course the chair was built Texas style, larger and broader than JFK's).

LBJ in his Texas-size rocker chats with Gina Lollobrigida.

*Kirk Douglas was the kind of
movie star LBJ could stomach.*

But there's only so much even an exceedingly powerful person can do to transfer his legend into popular culture. To spread and endure, a public image needs a great deal of investment from the public, an infusion of fantasy material based on a morbid fascination transmitted by receptive public media. From the start, the image Johnson hoped to transmit was often not the image that was received and disseminated. His blatant attempts to self-generate his myth struck the media as crass and usurpative—Johnson City will never look remotely like a city to any outsider.

Theodore White, explaining in 1961 why he believed Lyndon Johnson would never be elected president, said that he "presented himself as something essentially provincial." He continued:

To watch Lyndon B. Johnson perform oratory on his native heath is to see something like an act out of a show-boat production. . . . [His voice] roars like a bull's; it drops to a confidential whisper as he tells grassy jokes; it achieves a high-pitched Southern resonance. . . . [His face] seems a wad of India rubber—his mouth draws tight in anger, opens wide in a bellow of indignation, sucks in about the corners as he ruminates aloud, turns up in a great smile after the joke, turns down in sorrow as he wails of the nation's problems. When Lyndon B. Johnson is in good form and seen in the proper setting—say, at a small-town Masonic temple at a dinner for small-town Southern Democrats where the hot food is being served by the good Ladies of the Eastern Star—one can observe a master performance of native American political art. . . . [Elsewhere, or on tv] it has no smack of Presidential quality about it. It is, sadly, what is called in the cynical North and the citizen West "cornball." . . .

That same year, Mailer also condemned him with a brilliant caricature:

When he smiled the corners of his mouth squeezed gloom; when he was pious, his eyes twinkled irony; when he spoke in a righteous tone, he looked corrupt; when he jested, the ham in his jowls looked to quiver. He was not convincing. He was a

Southern politician, a Texas Democrat, a liberal Eisenhower. . . . The Russians would understand him better than his own.

Johnson cultivated few of the celebrity connections that might have lent some glamour to his earthy image. He didn't much like Hollywood and Hollywood didn't much like him. Brownstein relates that at a 1960 Hollywood fundraiser for the Kennedy-Johnson ticket attended by such stars as Joseph Cotton and Audrey Hepburn, "Johnson was bored. He stamped around the elegant room distractedly for ten minutes, and then . . . grumbled, 'Okay, let's go.'"

Similarly, Hedrick Smith reports in *The Power Game* that Johnson was uncomfortable at the annual Gridiron Club dinner, "one of the high tribal rites of Washington insiders." Every year top journalists gather at the Gridiron with Hollywood stars and Washington power brokers to enjoy a vaudevillian roast of the man in power. How well a politician handles the ribbing is said to have critical impact on his standing with the press. Johnson griped that the affair was "about as much fun as throwing cowshit at the village idiot."

Jack Valenti, the Johnson White House aide who went on to head the Motion Picture Association of America, told Brownstein that Johnson "was almost functionally illiterate about who stars were."

Indeed, the movies the Johnsons watched in the White House's private theater were more often about Washington and politics than Hollywood high life. A Johnson Library card file of movies they viewed lists *7 Days in May, Fail-Safe, In Harm's Way,* and several USIA documentary/propaganda films about Johnson trips and activities.

A large number of liberal celebrities did turn out in 1964 to campaign for Johnson against the nearly star-bereft Barry Goldwater. But over the next few years, with the Vietnam War dragging on and rioting in the streets, fewer and fewer stars cared to be associated with him. Eventually only the truly stalwart shmoozers, conservatives, and an odd lot of has-beens were left. A White House dinner for His Excellency Field Marshall Kittikachorn of Thailand, for example, was attended by James Brown, Danny Thomas, Arthur Godfrey and Dan Blocker. At Johnson "stag" dinners performers like Godfrey,

Ronnie and Donnie Copper, the Easter Seal Twins of 1964, stand on their heads for their president.

Gregory Peck and Burt Lancaster would mix it up with David Susskind, John Steinbeck, Roy Wilkins, cabinet chiefs and business leaders.

Johnson of course did have a few favorite stars. Not surprisingly, one was John Wayne. They were of a type: big, blustering, bad actors. Wayne made his movie *The Green Berets* to demonstrate his support of Johnson's war effort. Unfortunately, it was a very bad movie, made in 1968, which was too late to have done Johnson any good. Fellow Texan and cattleman Gregory Peck and his wife were frequent visitors both at the LBJ White House and the LBJ Ranch, where Peck and Johnson were photographed reclining like lovers in a field of black-eyed Susans. Peck campaigned for Johnson and narrated propaganda films for him. He and Hugh O'Brian appeared on Joey Bishop's tv show to express their support of Johnson's proposed gun-control legislation.

Curiously, when Johnson let Hollywood into his life, he let it way in. One of his earliest Hollywood contacts was Helen Gahagan Douglas, an actress and the wife of Melvyn Douglas. She gave up acting to become a liberal activist and was elected to Congress in 1944. She was a rising star among younger Democrats of the time, an early civil rights advocate and outspoken in her opposition to the proliferation of atomic weapons. She was even mentioned as a possible vice-presidential running mate for Harry Truman in 1948. LBJ advised Douglas in her campaigning—and, according to Califano, had an affair with her.

Although it's largely forgotten to political history, for about a year it looked like Lyndon Johnson might well become the father-in-law of a movie star: "Gorgeous" George Hamilton, the impeccably tanned caricature of the Hollywood playboy. While on one level he was the epitome of the frivolous, foppish Hollywood ne'er-do-wells Johnson had no time for, Hamilton did have a few things going for him: he was originally from the South, he was wealthy, and the Johnson ladies, mother as well as daughters, were utterly disarmed by his boyish looks and roguish charm.

Hamilton was among the celebrities who campaigned for Johnson in 1964. By late 1965 he and Lynda Bird were becoming a bona fide item. Popular magazines like the Sunday newspaper supplement *Parade* took to referring to him, in the stiffly quaint jargon writers often felt compelled to use in writing about the Johnsons, as her "beau."

Christmas at the LBJ ranch with the soon-to-be-banished almost-son-in-law.

He was in his mid-twenties, she just into her twenties. He attended White House receptions for foreign dignitaries and boated with the family on the *Honey Fitz*. He took Lynda Bird to the Academy Awards ceremony in Los Angeles and to Mardi Gras in New Orleans, and he was her date when she graduated from the University of Texas at Austin; afterwards they rode around town to various parties in a friend's antique fire engine.

Hamilton was a frequent overnight guest at the LBJ Ranch, where he and Lynda Bird would go riding and shooting. Sometimes he'd be flown there on Air Force One. He joined the Johnson family for Christmas Eve in 1966 and exchanged gifts with his almost-father-in-law. He made a spectacular entrance on New Year's Eve, flying in from London for the night's celebrations and flying back out the next day at noon. In her *White House Diary,* Lady Bird confessed to feeling a mother's trepidation about some of the fast running and high living George and Lynda Bird were doing, but she reminded herself that her daughter was, after all, now a grown woman of twenty-one.

Her qualms, it turned out, were the least of the young couple's problems. First *Parade,* and then the network news, revealed that at a time when Johnson was vastly escalating the flow of drafted troops into Vietnam, Hamilton, though fit to serve in the military, was avoiding service on a draft deferment, having claimed to be the sole source of support for his mother. His mother, the press pointed out, was a millionaire and living with him in his palatial movie star's mansion.

Scathing editorials appeared in many newspapers. The White House received a deluge of outraged letters and telegrams from the parents, spouses and girlfriends of boys who'd been drafted to fight in Vietnam. Hamilton only fanned the flames when he announced a plan to join a USO tour of Vietnam. To make matters worse, it dawned on the public and the press that Luci Bird's beau, Pat Nugent, was also safely shielded from harm as a National Guardsman.

Hamilton never did serve, and he soon vanished from the Johnson household. According to Lady Bird's diary, Lynda Bird woke her parents early one morning in 1967 to tell them that she had a new love. He was the polar opposite of Hamilton, a beau LBJ could have handpicked for her (and some suspected he did): crewcut, all-American, straight-arrow marine Chuck Robb.

The giant Texas rancher and the tiny former farm worker trade glares.

Another star who suffered a kind of banishment for her position on the war was Eartha Kitt. In November of 1968 she was a guest at Lady Bird's "Women Doers" luncheon to discuss what could be done about crime on the streets and the problem of youth violence. Other Women Doers included Mrs. Ramsey Clark, Mrs. Cyrus Vance, and New York judge Caroline Simon. Kitt listened to them chatter for a while about getting brighter street lamps and planting more flowers along the boulevards, and when she could take no more of it she stood up and harangued the ladies, accusing them of being privileged

Bob Hope and Jerry Colonna
do a little soft-shoe.

liberal wives who hadn't a clue what was going on. "I have lived in the gutters," she told them. "That's why I know what I am talking about." She brought Lady Bird to tears, telling her that at the root of youth crime was the despair of poverty and the unjust war her husband was promoting.

Her voice trembling, Lady Bird replied, "I am sorry I cannot understand as much as I should because I have not lived in the background as you have." Her husband, passing down the hallway between meetings, stuck his head in the door and caught the tail end of the confrontation. He and Kitt went at it briefly, lecturing each other in cold, furious tones, the giant Texas rancher looming over the tiny former farm worker, glaring at her with narrowed eyes in his trademark "serious-business" stare.

When it was over, Lady Bird demanded an explanation from her social-affairs secretary, Liz Carpenter, who'd invited Kitt. The Attorney General's office launched an inquiry into Kitt's background and prior political activities. A memo from Carpenter to the First Lady assured her that Kitt's record revealed no prior "peacenik activity" and added the appalling insinuation that Kitt was "not well thought of by her people. She had married a white man."

Kitt's outburst delighted antiwar protesters and some blacks, but the entertainment industry reacted with horror. Gregory Peck telegrammed the president to apologize on behalf of all entertainers for her bad behavior. Kitt's career all but vanished in the United States and was only dimly revived as a kind of nostalgia and novelty act in the late 1980s.

✦   ✦   ✦

Bob Hope, who'd been given a gold Medal of Freedom by JFK, lobbied hard but unsuccessfully to have LBJ give one to his friend Jack Benny. He also brought his pal Jerry Colonna to the Oval Office, where the two did a little shucking and jiving. He induced Ronnie and Donnie Copper, the Easter Seal Twins of 1964, to stand on their heads for their president. These scenes could not possibly be what Johnson meant when he wrote in a thank you letter that "If all the world were populated with Bob Hopes, what a good place it would be."

LBJ and Cantiflas had a special understanding.

LBJ was fond of the Mexican clown-actor Cantiflas. In November of 1965 Cantiflas and Billy Graham were guests at the LBJ Ranch and shared a porch swing with the presi-

dent; the day before, Cantiflas and LBJ had gone hunting, and Cantiflas bagged a deer. LBJ telephoned Cantiflas in Mexico City to wish him a happy New Year that December 30. They had an understanding, the Texas rancher and the Mexican clown.

Ultimately, it says a lot about Johnson's attitude toward celebrity that his two favorite show-business people were not actually entertainers but businessmen. One was Lew Wasserman of MCA, whom Brownstein calls "the last of the moguls," a major California fund raiser for LBJ (and later Jimmy Carter); the other was United Artists' Arthur Krim. Krim was also a powerful fund raiser for LBJ (and JFK previously), but more than that he became one of Johnson's closest friends and advisors. Brownstein quotes from a letter Johnson wrote to Krim: "I am always cheered when there is a Krim around." Krim was one of the first people Johnson told he wasn't going to run for reelection in 1968, and one of the last people he said goodnight to after he read the announcement on tv.

It may say everything about Hollywood's perception of LBJ that the Johnsons' prime time in the White House coincided with the Clampetts' prime time in the Hills of Beverly. LBJ never did shake the impression that his was a "Beverly Hillbillies" presidency. Years later, Jimmy Carter noted in his memoirs that "Lyndon Johnson went to his grave convinced that he was a victim of regional prejudice."

THE KING GOES INCOGNITO

AMONG HIS PEOPLE

No one, now, minds a con man.
But no one likes a con man who
doesn't know what we think we want.
George W. S. Trow

Early on the morning of December 21, 1970, Elvis Presley drove up to the northwest gate of the White House and handed the marine on guard there a letter he'd written to Nixon on the plane overnight. He'd flown not in his private jet, the *Lisa Marie*, but in a commercial airliner, one of the few times in his life he'd done so. He was dressed in a purple velvet pant suit and cape, with his signature high-collared shirt and belt buckle the size of a license plate, carrying a jeweled cane and a loaded .45 in a shoulder holster, wearing also perhaps the most famous face and hairdo in the world. He believed he was traveling incognito, and in the grand tradition of kings moving among their people, he adopted a pseudonym and rubbed elbows with the commoners, wanting to be known not as The King but simply as Jon Burrows or Dr. John Carpenter (the character he'd played the year before in the movie *Change of Habit*).

Neither Elvis nor the commoners he encountered quite had the hang of this kingly tradition, and all failed to play their parts. At the airport, according to Jerry Hopkins' *Elvis: The Final Years*, when The King was informed that he couldn't board the plane carrying his loaded pistol he threw a fit and stormed away from the gate. The pilot chased him down the hall, apologized profusely, and The King was wafted aboard, .45 and all.

Page 63. *Nixon and Elvis in the Oval Office.*

65

Stewardesses tripped over themselves to serve him. His fellow passengers similarly made no attempt to pretend they didn't recognize Elvis Presley.

The note Elvis wrote on board, on American Airlines stationery, begins:

Dear Mr. President:

First I would like to introduce myself. I am Elvis Presley and admire you and Have Great Respect for your office. I talked to Vice President agnew in Palm Springs 3 weeks ago and expressed my concern for our country. The Drug Culture, The Hippie Elements, the SDS, Black Panthers, etc do <u>not</u> consider me as their enemy or as they call it The Establishment. <u>I call it America and</u> I love it.

Elvis had previously met with John Finlator, deputy U.S. narcotics director, to ask for a federal narcotics agent's badge—partly because he really did seem to think he could help fight drugs in the entertainment industry, and partly because it would allow him to carry a gun anywhere in the country. (He had already gotten deputy sheriff's badges

from Memphis and elsewhere and had taken to arming himself at all times while at Graceland, supposedly even sleeping with a pistol tucked into the waistband of his pajamas.) Finlator had half-jokingly told him that the only man in the country who had the power to give him a fed's badge was the president. Instantly he flew to D.C. and had himself driven directly from the airport to the White House, where he dropped off his note for Nixon, in which he promised:

> *Sir I can and will be of any Service that I can to help the country out. . . . I have done an in depth study of Drug Abuse and Communist Brainwashing Techniques*

*and I am right in the middle of the whole thing, where I can and will do the
most good. . . .*

At some point that morning, White House staffer Dwight Chapin sent a two-page
memo to Nixon aide H. R. Haldeman (later convicted as a Watergate conspirator) noting
that "Presley showed up here this morning and has requested an appointment with the
President. He states that he knows the President is very busy, but he would just like to
say hello and present the President with a gift."

Chapin continued:

I have talked to Bud Korgh [sic] about this whole matter, and we both think that it would be wrong to push Presley off on the Vice President since it will take very little of the President's time and it can be extremely beneficial for the President to build some rapport with Presley.

In addition, if the President wants to meet with some bright young people out-side of the Government, Presley might be a perfect one to start with.

Haldeman wrote in the margin: *You must be kidding.* Nevertheless, the meeting was arranged for 12:30, the end of the president's scheduled "Open Hour" of brief visits for hand-shakes and photos. A briefing memo prepared for Nixon included such "Talking Points" as

We have asked the entertainment industry—both television and radio—to assist us in our drug fight.

You are aware that the average American family has 4 radio sets; 98% of the young people between 12 and 17 listen to radio. Between the time a child is born and he leaves high school, it is estimated he watches between 15,000 and 20,000 hours of television. That is more time than he spends in the classroom. . . .

Two of youth's folk heroes, Jimi Hendrix and Janis Joplin, recently died within a period of two weeks reportedly from drug-related causes. . . . If our youth are going to emulate the rock music stars, from now on let those stars affirm their conviction that true and lasting talent is the result of self motivation and disci-pline and not artificial chemical euphoria.

It goes on to suggest that Elvis, who had of course previously demonstrated a remarkable talent for maintaining a chemically induced euphoria, should "develop a new rock musical theme, 'Get High On Life,'" and record a live album by that name at the federal narcotics rehabilitation and research facility at Lexington, Kentucky.

At 12:30 that afternoon The King met the president in the Oval Office. Egil "Bud" Krogh, also later convicted as a Watergate conspirator, took notes and produced a memo reporting on the meeting:

*Presley immediately began showing the President his law enforcement parapher-
nalia including badges from police departments in California, Colorado and Tennessee. Presley indicated that he had been playing Las Vegas and the President
indicated that he was aware of how difficult it is to perform in Las Vegas. . . .*

*Presley indicated that he thought the Beatles had been a real force for anti-
American spirit. He said that the Beatles came to this country, made their money,
and then returned to England where they promoted an anti-American theme. The
President nodded in agreement and expressed some surprise. . . .*

*Presley indicated to the President in a very emotional manner that he was "on
your side." Presley kept repeating that he wanted to be helpful, that he wanted to
restore some respect for the flag which was being lost. He mentioned that he was
just a poor boy from Tennessee who had gotten a lot from his country, which in
some way he wanted to repay. He also mentioned that he is studying Communist
brainwashing and the drug culture for over ten years. He mentioned that he knew
a lot about this and was accepted by the hippies. He said he could go right into a
group of young people or hippies and be accepted which he felt could be helpful
to him in his drug drive. The President indicated again his concern that Presley
retain his credibility.*

*At the conclusion of the meeting, Presley again told the President how much
he supported him, and then, in a surprising, spontaneous gesture, put his left arm
around the President and hugged him.*

Krogh's memo doesn't mention other details revealed in the official photos. There
are the shots of Elvis giving Nixon a photo of himself and, evidently, a baby picture of
Lisa Marie. We also see Elvis showing the president his walletful of badges and the president admiring Elvis' cufflinks. According to Elvis lore, Nixon remarked, "Boy, you sure do
dress kind of wild."

At the end of the meeting, Elvis asked if Jerry and Red could come in and meet the
president too. He got the president to pose with them and give them both American flag
lapel pins. The King mentioned that they had wives and asked Nixon to give them American

December 31, 1970

Dear Mr. Presley:

It was a pleasure to meet with you in my office recently, and I want you to know once again how much I appreciate your thoughtfulness in giving me the commemorative World War II Colt 45 pistol, encased in the handsome wooden chest. You were particularly kind to remember me with this impressive gift, as well as your family photographs, and I am delighted to have them for my collection of special mementos.

With my best wishes to you, Mrs. Presley, and to your daughter, Lisa, for a happy and peaceful 1971.

Sincerely,

RICHARD NIXON

Mr. Elvis Presley
Box 417
Madison, Tennessee 37115

RN/lf/cf/cf   gift

The Presley pistol is now on display at the Nixon Library, one of its most popular exhibits.

Lucy:

Elvis Presley (believe it or not) was
granted an appointment with the President
on Monday, Dec. 21. He left these
autographed photos with the President.
I don't think any acknowledgment would
be necessary. For your good disposition!

Bev.

Rec'd. gun previously —

flag brooches to take home.* In return, Elvis gave the president the gold-plated .45 and bullets now on display at the Nixon Library & Birthplace in Yorba Linda.

Nixon instructed Krogh to get Elvis his federal drug agent's badge. It was delivered that afternoon.

Later, in one of his unconsciously self-referential pronouncements, Nixon would say that "Elvis had the power over people's imaginations that would enable him to attain high office."

Not surprisingly, Nixon subscribed to the argument that Kennedy stole the 1960 election from him simply because he looked better on tv. In *RN*, his massive memoirs published in 1975, he opines:

---

* A few years later, the newly installed President Ford sent aides to California to negotiate with Nixon the terms of his Watergate pardon. They were shocked to see how physically and mentally diminished he seemed. Nixon embarrassed them by insisting on giving them pins, too, only to discover that he had none left. To their horror, he sent for his jewelry case, and gave them what appeared to be his own last set.

It is a devastating commentary on the nature of television as a political medium that what hurt me the most in the first debate was not the substance of the encounter between Kennedy and me, but the disadvantageous contrast in our physical appearances. . . . As for television debates in general I doubt that they can ever serve a responsible role in defining the issues of a presidential campaign. Because of the nature of the medium, there will inevitably be a greater premium on showmanship than on statesmanship.

At best this is disingenuous. Nixon's relationships with television, Hollywood and the news media were as complex and devious as any other aspect of his odd career. While he constantly complained about how he was "shafted" by the media and cold-shouldered by celebrities, few politicians of his era matched his cynical opportunism in manipulating the media to improve his image and advance his career.

Early in his political career he used Hollywood, though in a typically twisted way, to promote himself to national visibility. In *The Power and The Glitter,* Brownstein describes how as a newly elected congressman in 1947-48 Nixon drew attention to himself with his participation in the first, and failed, House Un-American Activities Committee hearings into Communist influence in Hollywood.

In 1949 he ran for Senate against Democratic candidate Helen Gahagan Douglas, the former actress LBJ had befriended. Douglas' opponent in the Senate primary had labeled her "the pink lady," a sobriquet Nixon picked up and ran with as her Republican opponent in the general election. He distributed "pink sheets" distorting Douglas' liberal record and called her "pink right down to her underwear." He scorned the whole notion of Hollywood actors entering politics. Los Angeles newspapers picked up on the "pink lady" theme, and Nixon not only crushed her in the election but ended her career for good.

One of the few Hollywood figures who risked supporting Douglas was Ronald Reagan, who'd not yet completed the transition from liberal Democrat to conservative Republican. In his memoirs of the LBJ White House, Joseph Califano says that Johnson's despisal of Nixon dated back to his vicious trouncing of Douglas in 1949. "She was a fine

A pre–Star Wars Carrie Fisher seems to be wondering how she let her mom (Debbie Reynolds) drag her here.

President Nixon upstaged by the official Thanksgiving Turkey.

person," Califano quotes him as saying, "and he destroyed her."

Much as Nixon would later claim to have been ill-treated by television, he used it as early as 1952 to salvage his already scandal-ridden career when he made the infamously shmaltzy "Checkers" speech to defend himself against allegations of graft and greed. It worked and he went on to triumph as Eisenhower's vice president and continued to use television successfully, as in his famous washers-and-dryers debate with Nikita Krushchev.

In fact, it was Nixon's handlers, not Kennedy's, who dominated the stage management of their debates. Of all his political contemporaries, Nixon had the least claim to media innocence and the least excuse to blame television for favoring Kennedy's image over his. As tv critic Richard Schickel put it many years later, "It was not just a case of Kennedy being more attractive than Nixon. Who wasn't? . . ."

As later events proved, if Nixon looked shifty and twitchy in the Kennedy debate, it's because he *was* shifty and twitchy, not because tv made him look that way. At the time, however, few analysts understood that his failure to fool the tv cameras was no reason to condemn the medium; rather it represented one of television's few shining moments. By 1968 Nixon would become much more adept at lying to the camera, but in 1960, despite years of prior practice, he looked as untrustworthy as he was—looked, as Marshall McLuhan put it, like "the railway lawyer who signs leases that are not in the best interests of the folks in the little town."

Before Nixon learned how to hide the con man inside him, he would have to suffer a few more years of media abuse. In his unsuccessful 1962 run for governor of California he believed the news people had treated him so poorly that he refused to go before them to make a concession speech. He sent a flak instead and remained sulking in his hotel room. The news people hooted down the flak and demanded that Nixon come out and face them. When at last he did, he was so incensed that he blurted out one of the most baldly neurotic public addresses of his career:

> Now that all the members of the press are so delighted that I have lost, I'd like to
> make a statement. . . . And as I leave the press, all I can say is this: for sixteen

A White House visit from prelate Catholicos Khoren I.

RN, PN, and Rev. Graham do their impression of Mt. Rushmore.

The Pat Boones greet the Richard Nixons on the White House lawn.

years, ever since the Hiss case, you've had a lot of—a lot of fun—that you've had an opportunity to attack me. . . . But as I leave you I want you to know—just think how much you're going to be missing.

You won't have Nixon to kick around anymore, because, gentlemen, this is my last press conference, and it will be one in which I have welcomed the opportunity to test wits with you. I have always respected you. I have sometimes disagreed with you. But unlike some people, I've never cancelled a subscription to a paper, and also I never will. . . .

I hope that what I have said today will at least make television, radio, and the press . . . recognize that they have a right and a responsibility, if they're against a candidate, to give him the shaft, but also recognize that if they give him the

THE WHITE HOUSE

WASHINGTON

July 31, 1972

MEMORANDUM FOR: THE PRESIDENT

FROM: KEN COLE

SUBJECT: Photo with The Carpenters
                   Tuesday, August 1, 1972
                   12 Noon
                   President's Office
                   (5 Minutes)

I.   PURPOSE

     To greet a young talented "All American" recording
     group who have been involved voluntarily in the
     cancer field.

II. BACKGROUND, PARTICIPANTS, PRESS PLANS

     A. Background: The Carpenters are in town for
         an appearance at the Merriweather Post Pavilion
         at Columbia. They are a brother-sister recording
         group. Karen Carpenter is National Youth
         Chairman of the American Cancer Society. They
         donate all of the royalities from the sale of
         programs at their concerts to cancer research.
         $25,000 was donated 6 months ago. They now
         have an additional $35,000 to contribute.

     B. Participants: Karen Carpenter
                        Richard Carpenter

                        Staff: Ken Cole
                                Jim Cavanaugh

```
                                                    2

    C.  Press Plan:  To be announced: photo opportunity
        (Press to be told that the President heard about
        their work in the cancer field and wanted to
        personally congratulate them on their efforts.

III.  POINTS OF DISCUSSION

    A.  You should tell them that you have heard about
        their contributions to support cancer research
        and wanted to personally express the appreciation
        of the Nation for the fine example they have set.

    B.  You should mention that Julie told you about
        meeting them when they were here for lunch and
        a tour in April.

    C.  You should tell them what a great job Julie has
        been doing traveling across the country meeting
        with groups involved in voluntary activities
        with the Cancer Society.
```

shaft, put one lonely reporter on the campaign who will report what the candidate says now and then. . . .

Nixon continued to sulk for the next few years. He brooded enviously while his old nemesis LBJ occupied the White House and groused about "the martyr halo which Johnson was able to clutch to his brow" after Kennedy's assassination.

By 1968 he'd well learned the lessons of 1960 and 1962. He campaigned against Hubert Humphrey with a completely overhauled, tightly controlled tv image, hogging the airwaves with prefab messages but insulated from the press. His was the pioneering model for tv politics as it would be played for the next two decades. Humphrey, playing it straight, open with the press to the point of garrulousness, didn't stand a chance.

Joe McGinnis documented Nixon's 1968 media blitz with pitiless sarcasm in *The Selling of the President 1968.* The candid comments of Nixon's media handlers reveal

that these men were well aware they were plotting the descent into the future, but what rings clear in their comments is not so much a political cynicism as professional excitement at the challenge of designing a winning ad campaign against the odds of a loser product.

Raymond K. Price, a former journalist turned Nixon campaign speechwriter, wrote a memo in which he noted (his emphasis): "*We have to be very clear on this point: that the response is to the image, not to the man....* It's not what's *there* that counts, it's what's projected—and carrying it one step further, it's not what *he* projects but rather what the voter receives. It's not the man we have to change, but rather the *received impression.*" William Gavin, another speechwriter, stressed that Nixon had "to come across as a person larger than life, the stuff of legend. People are stirred by the legend, including the living legend, not by the man himself. It's the aura that surrounds the charismatic figure more than it is the figure itself...." Jim Sage, an assistant filmmaker who worked on Nixon's tv commercials, was one of the few team members who seemed troubled by moral doubt, which he cloaked in condescension in order to distance himself:

> *You know ... what we're really seeing here is a genesis. We're moving into a period where a man is going to be merchandised on television more and more. It upsets you and me, maybe, but we're not typical Americans. The public sits home and watches "Gunsmoke" and when they're fed this pap about Nixon they think they're getting something worthwhile.*
>
> *We didn't have to make cheap and vulgar films, you know. We're capable of doing more.... But those images strike a note of recognition in the kind of people to whom we are trying to appeal. The kind of person who might vote for Nixon in the first place.*

Nixon's tv ads were designed by Harry Treleaven, an executive from the J. Walter Thompson agency, where his accounts included RCA, Ford, Pan Am and Lark cigarettes. Before Nixon, he had worked on George Bush's bid for representative of Texas in 1966. Another member of the Nixon tv crew had worked on "Laugh-In." But the complete

The Carpenters, "a brother-sister recording group" with the wholesome, glassy-eyed image Nixon liked.

Johnny Cash lobbied Nixon for prison reforms.

THE WHITE HOUSE   Briefing Paper

WASHINGTON

July 25, 1972

MEMORANDUM FOR THE PRESIDENT

FROM: WILLIAM E. TIMMONS

SUBJECT: Meeting with Johnny Cash and
                         Sen. Bill Brock (R-Tenn)
                         Wednesday, July 26, 1972
                         12:00 - 12:05 p.m.
                         The President's Office

I.   PURPOSE

      To permit Johnny Cash to discuss his testimony before the Senate
      Subcommittee on National Penitentiaries on behalf of the Federal
      Corrections Reorganization Act, which is co-sponsored by
      Senators Brock, Percy and Montoya.

II.   BACKGROUND, PARTICIPANTS AND PRESS PLAN

      A. Background: Senator Brock requested that you meet with Johnny
         Cash. Cash has entertained inmates at many prisons and has
         become concerned about the persistent problems of "corrections."
         He is testifying before a Senate Judiciary Subcommittee on
         prison reform.

         Cash, who is friendly toward the Administration, is being asked
         to actively support your re-election and has been invited to join
         the Celebrities for the Re-Election of the President. You might
         want to ask him if he is interested in coming to the Convention
         and participating in some way. He has been reluctant sofar.

      B. Participants: Participants will include the President, Johnny
         Cash, Sen. Bill Brock and Bill Timmons. (Mrs. Cash -- June
         Carter -- will be in the West Lobby but does not intend to parti-
         cipate in the meeting. It would be a nice gesture to ask to meet
         Mrs. Cash again).

      C. Press Plan: To be announced with a press photo opportunity.

repackaging of the new Nixon for tv was masterminded by Roger Ailes, who was hired away from the "Mike Douglas Show" to create Nixon's phony, meticulously staged town hall discussions with small groups of carefully handpicked citizens.

Ailes, who went on to become a celebrity himself as media master nonpareil of the Reagan-Bush era, summed up Nixon in an interview with Joe McGinnis:

> *Let's face it, a lot of people think Nixon is dull. Think he's a bore, a pain in the ass. They look at him as the kind of kid who always carried a bookbag. Who was 42 years old the day he was born. . . .*
>
> *Now you put him on television, you've got a problem right away. He's a funny-looking guy. He looks like somebody hung him in a closet overnight and he jumps out in the morning with his suit all bunched up and starts running around saying, "I want to be President. "*

Nixon remained as isolated in the White House as he'd been on the campaign trail. Meanwhile, he built on what JFK and LBJ had begun in the way of information control and image manipulation. The result is that his own secret tapes, or what little the public has been allowed to hear—as of 1993, only 60 out of 950 hours' worth—continue to be the most intimate and revealing documents available on his life in the White House. Nixon's motivation for the taping, Seymour M. Hersh reported in a 1992 *New Yorker* article, was, ironically, to have "compelling material for a best-selling Presidential memoir. Nixon also saw the documents as a cash asset. Ehrlichman has written of a 1971 Oval Office conversation in which the President estimated that his personal papers would have a value of at least a dollar per page. 'Some may be worth more,' Erhlichman quoted Nixon as saying, 'but even my old laundry lists and grocery bills will be worth that much.'" The final irony, of course, is that in the wake of Watergate, Congress refused Nixon access to the tapes or any of his papers.

Nixon seemed more at ease with Bob Hope than with any other celebrity . . .

The Nixon White House did not hum with celebrity visitors. Elvis, though technically not an invited guest, clearly tops the list, which was not overweighted with glamour: Art Linkletter, Roberta Peters, Pat Boone, Glen Campbell, Tony Bennett, the Carpenters and Burl Ives were typical guests.

And of course there was Bob Hope. Nixon was more relaxed in Hope's presence than with any other celebrities, and vice versa. Whereas Hope had been reduced to shucking and jiving in LBJ's White House and felt compelled to go into shmooze overdrive with Ford, he comfortably offered Nixon friendly counsel and moral support.

It was Richard Nixon who finally gave Frank Sinatra his long-sought entrée to the White House. In *RN*, Nixon reports that Sinatra, "in his first appearance at the White House, had tears in his eyes when he thanked me afterward."

. . . and he discussed world affairs with him while they polished putts on the White House lawn.

Sammy Davis, Jr., another aging and presumably reforming member of the Rat Pack, was a major Nixon shmoozer. Nixon recalls him singing and dancing, and that "Sammy and his wife spent the night with us after his performance and—in fulfillment of a life-long dream—he slept in the Lincoln Bedroom." One of the funniest gifts on display at the Nixon Library & Birthplace—aside from a rock shaped like Nixon's head given to him by Barry Goldwater—is an enormous gold chain with a circular medallion roughly the circumference of a truck headlight on which, in hippiesque "Laugh-In" lettering, are the words PEACE AND LOVE, SAMMY.

By the 1972 presidential campaign, Nixon's celebrity faithful were down to John Wayne, Jack Benny, Sinatra, Georgie Jessel, Connie Francis and Jackie Gleason, whose taped pitch for him recorded in Miami read, "My name is Jackie Gleason and I love this country. I've never made a public choice like this before—but I think this country needs Dick Nixon and we need him now."

After Elvis, the most unlikely famous visitor to the Nixon White House may have been André Malraux, the writer, philosopher, resistance leader and France's Minister of Culture. Malraux had been a great admirer of the Kennedys, especially Jacqueline. Nixon could not have hoped to have lived up to that. Still, before making his trip to China he asked Malraux to the White House to share his insights into the character and motivations of Chairman Mao. Malraux told Nixon that Mao knew he was dying and that

meeting with the president of the United States would be his last historic act. "You may think he is talking to you," Malraux told Nixon, "but he will in truth be addressing Death."

Above. *Nixon, like Johnson before him, borrowed some of John Wayne's patriotic luster.*

When Soviet leader Leonid Brezhnev visited the United States in 1973, Nixon first met with him at Camp David. Nixon's people had found out that Brezhnev admired big, fancy American cars, so Nixon arranged for him to be given a Lincoln Continental. A delighted Brezhnev proceeded to alarm Secret Service people and White House staff by driving it

Opposite. *Sammy Davis, Jr., not singing or dancing.*

Golfing in Florida with another supporter, Jackie Gleason.

like a madman all over Camp David's wooded, hilly grounds.

The festivities then moved to the Western White House at San Clemente, where the Nixons threw a soiree. "I am here in the home of President and Mrs. Nixon," Brezhnev toasted, "and I feel happy." Strolling mariachi bands played. Numerous Republican movie stars came out to mill around the pool and nibble on canapés. Sinatra was there. Ronald Reagan was there, too, and the staff photographer caught some wonderful body language when he, Brezhnev and Nixon huddled in a quiet corner of the patio having what looks like a brooding tête-à-tête through an interpreter at Brezhnev's shoulder.

Brezhnev received a much warmer reception from another cowboy actor, Chuck Connors. A big fan of "The Rifleman," Brezhnev had specifically asked to meet Connors. Connors and Brezhnev got along famously. Their camaraderie was instantaneous and almost unseemly—they hugged each other, gave each other playful punches and squeezes on the arm, cracked each other up with jokes. The image of Connors arming Brezhnev with six-guns and teaching him the quick draw captures a bizarrely symbolic gesture of Cold War codependence, complete with Brezhnev's acquiescing to wearing the black hat. The next day, in a much-publicized farewell scene on the runway as Brezhnev was about to fly home, Connors lifted the Soviet premiere off his feet in a hearty bear hug.

Having once likened Richard Nixon to Shakespeare's Richard the Third, Richard Schickel resorted to more modern show-biz metaphors to sum up Nixon's role in American political mythology:

> As politics turned into megatheater we needed him as our dark star, the visible manifestation of the dingy side of the American character, that side which has always relished frauds, cons, scams, and especially envies, even admires, people who keep pulling them off. He was, perhaps, the W. C. Fields or the Willie Sutton of politics—though without the former's comic genius or the bank robber's insouciant charm. . . . It may be, indeed, as David T. Bazelon has speculated, that no nation achieves maturity without first enduring the reign of some figure who encapsulates and forces it to contemplate the most evil aspects of its nature—Ivan the Terrible, Napoleon, Mussolini, Hitler. If that be so then we were lucky; Nixon was a far more paltry figure than any of those monsters of the grand scale.

The Rifleman arms Soviet leader Brezhnev, the one in the black hat.

THE PEACESTONE

PRESIDENT

My God, this is going to change our whole life.
Betty Ford

In his day Gerald Ford was universally lampooned as a dullard, a bumbler forever tripping over his own feet or his own tongue. Irritated by Congressman Ford's stolid Republican resistance to Great Society spending proposals, LBJ launched an insult into popular usage when he joked that Gerald Ford couldn't walk and chew gum at the same time; he also speculated that he'd played too much football without a helmet in college. The most famous news footage of his presidency was of him losing his footing, skiing backwards, getting tongue-tied and so on.

Ford's mercifully short time in the White House was the most hapless and accident-prone of modern presidencies, including Carter's. But how much of the ridicule was anger at Nixon spilling over to him, a guilt by association that Ford, with characteristic clumsiness, accepted when he instantly pardoned Nixon and left the nation with a bad case of regicide interruptus? If Nixon ultimately managed to weasel out of our grasp, at least we could nab his surrogate in the act of embarrassing himself. Ford's swift pardoning of Nixon achieved exactly the opposite effect of what he had intended: instead of "healing the nation" it intensified the public's mistrust of insider politics that would later float Carter and then Reagan into office.

Perhaps this displaced anger was in part responsible for the two surprising attempts on Ford's life—both by women in California, and both in September 1975. Appropriately, both Squeaky Fromme and Sara Jane Moore bungled their chances to assassinate the

Page 99. *Hike!*

bumbler president. Maybe they missed because they weren't really aiming at him but at some Nixonian ghost hovering near him. When Squeaky was arrested, she shouted, "This man is not your president!" Maybe she meant it literally.

Lynette Alice "Squeaky" Fromme, twenty-six years old, former Manson family member, made her attempt in Sacramento on September 6, 1975. Ford had just given an address before the California state legislature—his topic was crime in America—and he was walking from the Senator Hotel toward Governor Jerry Brown's office, shaking hands with the crowd along the way. "I spotted a woman in a bright red dress," he writes in his memoirs. "She was in the second or third row, moving right along with me as if she wanted to shake my hand. When I slowed down, I noticed immediately that she thrust her hand under the arms of the other spectators. I reached down to shake it—and looked into the barrel of a .45 caliber pistol pointed directly at me." (A White House staffer walking beside the president reported that Ford's face "went blank with shock or surprise.")

The gun misfired. "It didn't go off. Can you believe it?" Squeaky asked the

The president reached out to shake Squeaky's hand, but there was a gun in it.

cops and Secret Service agents who dragged her away. They could believe it: her gun was an ancient .45 caliber service revolver that had been sold as army surplus as early as 1913.

Ford strolled on to his meeting with Jerry Brown. The meeting lasted forty minutes, during which Ford never mentioned that someone had just tried to kill him. When a puzzled aide asked him why not, Ford merely shrugged and replied that the subject "had never come up."

As her sentence to life in prison was being read, Squeaky bounced an apple off the prosecutor's head and yelled at the judge: "I held up the gun and said don't make me shoot. You kept saying 'Do it, do it, do it.' I think I have done all I can save killing you. You fool, I'm just trying to save your life. The International People's Court of Retribution will give you what you deserve."

Sara Jane Moore took her shot just two weeks later, on September 22, in San Francisco, as Ford was exiting the St. Francis Hotel. "Bang!" Ford later wrote. "I recognized the sound of a shot, and I froze. There was a hushed silence for a split second. Then pandemonium broke out." He was bustled off to the airport, where Betty was waiting for him aboard Air Force One. Unaware of what had happened, she asked him how his day had gone.

Moore, a middle-aged mother and multiple divorcée, was an informer inside Bay Area radical groups for both the feds and local cops. She had a long history of emotional problems and had once turned up on the streets of D.C., very near the White House, wandering around in a state of amnesia. She had been detained by the authorities the day before she shot at Ford. They had taken a gun away from her and she had warned them that she had entertained thoughts of killing the president "to test the system." They let her go free anyway. She went out the next day, bought another gun, and took her shot.

She missed because "an alert ex-marine," as the wire services at first described him, deflected her arm. The ex-marine, Oliver Sipple, was originally from Ford's home state of Michigan. You'd think the two of them might have traveled home together triumphantly—a parade in Detroit maybe, a public bestowing of a medal on the heroic young man, something. But this is where the Ford fumble factor turned tragic.

Instead, Ford shunned the man who'd saved his life. At the Ford Library there seems to be not a single mention of Oliver Sipple in several fat file boxes of White House materials regarding the assassination attempt. Sipple was living an openly gay life in San Francisco—a fact he'd kept hidden from his folks back home in Detroit—and when the reporters discovered it, Sipple begged them not to write about it (though some did anyway).

Ford's advisors evidently decided it wouldn't be good for the president to associate in public with a gay man. Sipple's mother was heartbroken when she learned of her son's lifestyle. When she died in 1979 Sipple's father wouldn't allow him to attend her funeral.

Sergeant Barry Sadler, who'd had a hit years before with "The Ballad of the Green Berets," playing a tape of a new song for the president. This one was not a hit.

Sipple had by then become an alcoholic, and he drank himself to death a few months later, at the age of thirty-seven.

The same year that Ford reached out, he thought, to shake Squeaky's hand and saw there was a gun in it, he also unknowingly touched the hand of a successful assassin. On a visit to a YMCA facility in Fort Chaffee, Arizona, he shook hands with Mark David Chapman, who later killed John Lennon.

Ford's bungling and clumsiness may be a side-effect of his odd ambidexterity. Ford believes this had something to do with a period of stuttering he experienced as a child (and from which he clearly never fully recovered). As he noted in his memoirs, "For as long as I can remember, I have been left-handed when I've been sitting down and right-handed standing up. As strange as this may sound, I'd throw a football with my right hand and write with my left."

Jerry and Bob on the greens.

He was always the man in the middle, the man who would *not* be king. In his memoirs he claimed that the presidency was "a job to which I'd never aspired." His highest ambition had been to be the Speaker of the House, and with Congress still in the grip of LBJ Democrats, he was considering retirement when Nixon tapped him to replace the disgraced Agnew as vice president. He'd been the last name on a roster of more colorful candidates including Ronald Reagan, Nelson Rockefeller and John Connally, who were either smart enough to

No wonder he stumbled. No wonder he played center on the University of Michigan football team. No wonder he was the quintessential centrist as a politician. He built his congressional career as a moderator and compromiser. As president, he pardoned Nixon, but he was also the first to float the idea of pardoning Vietnam War draft dodgers. He later wrote that he "tried to show leadership by projecting a calm and steady hand." (Which one?) "Some people misinterpreted this by concluding that we were stodgy and unimaginative, but that didn't bother me."

turn down the offer or too smart for Nixon to feel comfortable with them. When Nixon resigned and Ford was informed he'd have to step up, Betty Ford exclaimed, "My God, this is going to change our whole life."

Ford was well aware he was an unelected, caretaker president. He downplayed his role like a man who knew he didn't own the Big Chair but was only renting it. In *A Time to Heal* he writes:

> *A pioneer family would struggle for years to pay off the mortgage on their home. Once the final payment was made, they'd place a special stone above the fireplace or in the newel post of the stairs. They'd call it a "peacestone" and its presence would signify that the home was theirs at last. In August 1974, my ambition was to put the peacestone back in the foundation of America.*

Presidents traditionally complain about the burdens of the office, the crushing responsibilities, the murderous workload. Taft called the White House "the loneliest place in the world." Harding called the Oval Office "a prison."

Ford, on the other hand, found the Oval Office "large, comfortable and inspiring. I knew there were many far-reaching things that I as President could do, but I never sat in the chair behind my desk and said, 'I'm a powerful man. I can press a button or pull a switch and such and such will happen.'" When people asked him if the burden of leadership kept him up all night, Ford says he would reply, " 'Absolutely not.' I never felt better physically. I never had a clearer mind."

And he partied. It's been said that Gerald and Betty Ford threw the most fun White House parties in modern times. It might even be said that Betty's lasting mark on posterity is as a patron saint of recovering partyers. Perhaps they suspected, like JFK before them, that they were short-timers and needed to get all their living in quick. Or maybe to fill the vacuum of their nonimage, they surrounded themselves with celebrities. Though the Ford years are always characterized as extraordinarily dull, on closer inspection the Fords' two and a half years in the White House appear to have been one long shmoozathon. The Fords and their children, who were then at peak partying age, were

Marty Allen and Betty do the bump.

virtually barnacled with movie stars, rock stars and lesser hacks of all types. It's not just the long lists of celebrity names attached to them that are impressive, but the *intensity* of the shmoozing that went on.

There was undoubtedly a special chemistry between Ford and singer Vikki Carr, for instance. She visited the Ford White House several times. They certainly appear to be flirting in the photos taken of them dancing during a state dinner for Austrian Prime

Above. *Nurse Geraldine pays off Flip Wilson's golfing debt.*

Opposite. *Clockwise from top left: Nanette Fabray; Wayne Newton says "Danke Schön"; Telly Savalas; the Jimmy Stewarts.*

Minister Bruno Kreisky in 1975. Carr's dress is practically indistinguishable from lingerie (prefiguring, in a manner of speaking, Madonna's underwear look of the eighties). In *A Time to Heal*, Ford tells of the first time they'd met a year earlier:

> *She is of Mexican descent, and when I congratulated her on her performance, she offered to invite me to her home in Los Angeles for dinner sometime soon. "What Mexican dish do you like?" she asked me. I looked at her and cracked, "I like you." Betty overheard the exchange, and needless to say, she wasn't wild about it.*

Despite the dull impression he invariably made on the public, Ford in private was evidently a hit with many ladies. The Ford Library is filled with photos of pretty women openly flirting with him, from aging actresses to young women and coeds hugging him, kissing him, hanging from his broad shoulders, throwing him ravishing looks. No president since JFK seems to have basked in so much feminine attention. Obviously enjoying it, Ford looks surprisingly handsome, even dashing in a fatherly or older-manly way. Power is sexy, and to be the most powerful man in the world is most sexy.

Joe Garagiola was certainly smitten with Ford. In the summer of 1976 they shared a box at the All-Star Game. Garagiola's letter to Ford after the event oozes with the tremulous gushings of a morning-after love note. "I haven't stopped thinking about that great night. . . ." he wrote. "Somehow, some way I believe you know how I feel."

On election night the following November, Joe was an honorary family member, watching the returns with them in their private quarters, sharing the couch with the president. They watched NBC because its election map showed the states going for Carter in red and those going for Ford in blue. "Big Blue" was the nickname of the University of Michigan football team, and Joe and Jerry cheered at the screen: "Go, Big Blue!"

But Big Blue was not a goer. Ford writes that midway through the long night, when the whole southern half of the map had turned red, "Garagiola came up and put his hand on my shoulder. 'It's all right, Prez,' he said. 'We've given up a couple of runs, but the ball game is only in the top of the fourth; we got a long way to go.'"

Vikki Carr and President Ford.

Joe Garagiola looking disconsolate as Ford loses the 1976 election.

As the ball game proceeded, Garagiola looked increasingly crestfallen and distraught. Sitting next to him, smoking a pipe, Ford looked resigned and philosophical. By the next morning, it was over. Ford wrote,

[We] threw our arms around each other without saying a word, because nothing needed to be said. For as long as I live, I won't forget that scene. There we were, two has-been athletes, hugging each other in total silence. Then the mood broke and the tears began to flow. "Damn it, we shoulda won. We shoulda won," he said.
    I tried to comfort him. . . .

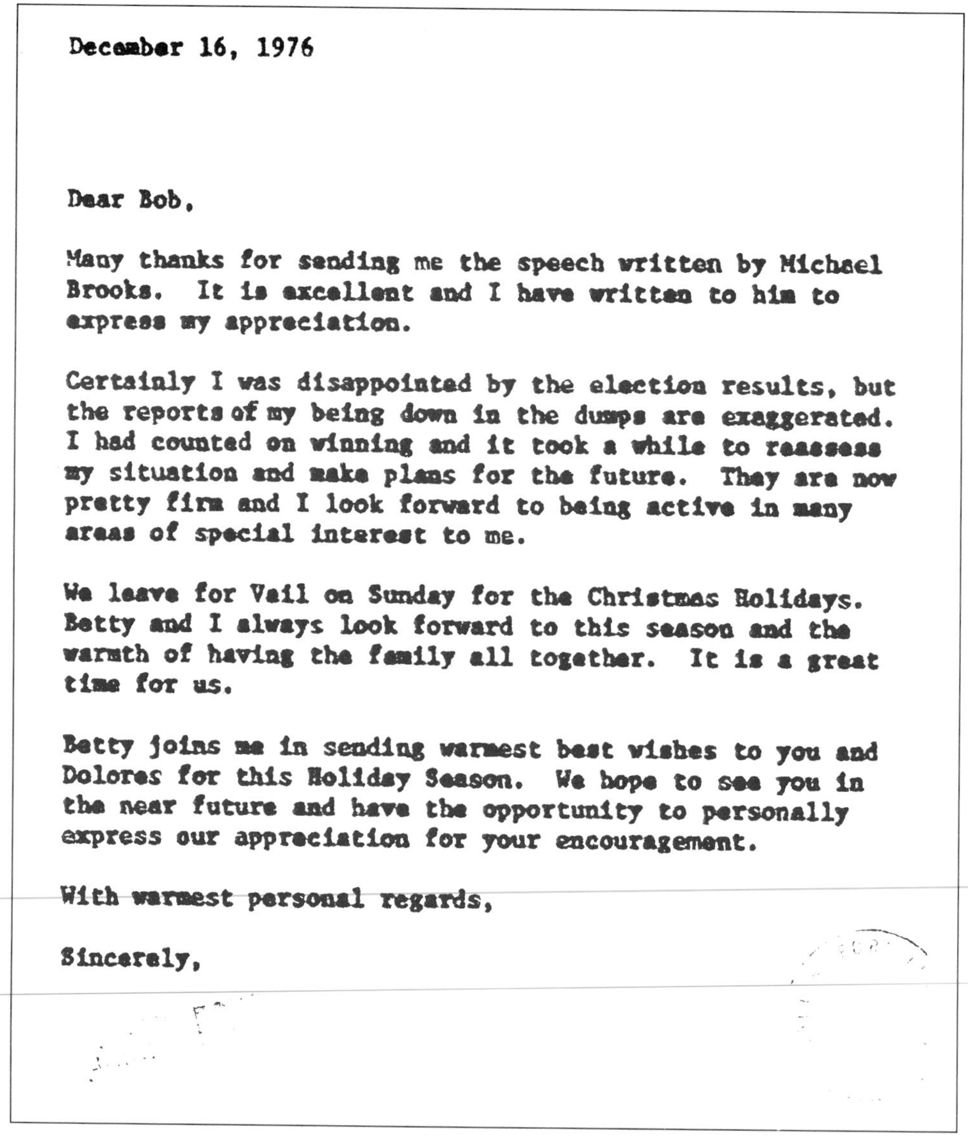

December 16, 1976

Dear Bob,

Many thanks for sending me the speech written by Michael Brooks. It is excellent and I have written to him to express my appreciation.

Certainly I was disappointed by the election results, but the reports of my being down in the dumps are exaggerated. I had counted on winning and it took a while to reassess my situation and make plans for the future. They are now pretty firm and I look forward to being active in many areas of special interest to me.

We leave for Vail on Sunday for the Christmas Holidays. Betty and I always look forward to this season and the warmth of having the family all together. It is a great time for us.

Betty joins me in sending warmest best wishes to you and Dolores for this Holiday Season. We hope to see you in the near future and have the opportunity to personally express our appreciation for your encouragement.

With warmest personal regards,

Sincerely,

The Ford family, sans Joe, then went on tv to announce his concession. Gerald Ford did not read his concession speech himself. He and Joe had yelled themselves hoarse the night before. Betty read it for him.

Bob Hope wasted no time seeking to set the tone of the relationship he wanted with Ford. Nixon resigned on August 8, 1974; Ford pardoned him on September 8; September 9 Hope sent Ford a telegram that began BRAVO. APPROVE OF YOUR ACTION. Evidently unaware that their administration required Hope's approval, Ford's staff was diffident at first. They strongly argued that Ford's appearance in a Dean Martin tv roast of Bob Hope would be in "bad taste" and, considering Hope's close ties with Nixon and Agnew, worse politics. Apparently they forgot to inform the producer of the show, who sent a crew to Washington.

Nurtured by their common interest in golf and fertilized with relentless ingratiation, Hope's relationship with Ford blossomed after that. In July of 1975 he sent Ford a birthday telegram: 62 AIN'T BAD THAT'S 10 UNDER PAR CONGRATULATIONS

At the Vail ski resort the following Christmas, the Fords received a "beautiful topiary tree" sent by Bob and Dolores Hope. The following spring, when the Fords went to Los

Ford golfing with lounge lizard Phil Harris.

THE WHITE HOUSE

WASHINGTON

October 14, 1974

No

MEMORANDUM FOR: RON NESSEN

FROM: BOB ME___

SUBJECT: Dean Martin Roast of Bob Hope

It would be my recommendation that the President should not participate in the "roasting" of Bob Hope on the Dean Martin Show. (First of 6 specials).

Besides being a great demand on his busy schedule (since NBC wants it done before October 18th), I don't think it is an appropriate appearance, at this time, when the President is talking seriously on such matters as inflation and the economy, the Nixon pardon, etc., and the upcoming elections.

1.) At this time, it would be in poor taste.

2.) Jokes written and delivered now could be outdated by air time, which is about 3 weeks away, October 31st.

3.) Professional joke tellers and comedians could make him look uneasy and too unprofessional.

4.) There was criticism of Richard Nixon when he appeared on "Laugh-In" on NBC and he wasn't President at that time.

5.) Even though Bob Hope has been a friend of "all" Presidents, his indentification with former President Nixon strongly lingers; he still plays golf with Agnew; and is not a personal friend of the President, nor has a friendship been publicly established.

6.) "To honor" and "to roast" are separate identities.

7.) Signed for the show so far are: Howard Cosell, Phyllis Diller, Jack Benny, James Stewart, Ronald Reagan.

S-G PRODUCTIONS

3630 RIVERSIDE DRIVE ● BURBANK, CALIFORNIA 91505

TELEPHONE 849-2471

November 11, 1974

Mr. Robert T. Hartmann
The White House
Washington, D.C.

Dear Mr. Hartmann:

I'm sorry it didn't work for the Bob Hope Roast and I know
how cooperative you were on our behalf, and I thank you for
that. You're a good man, Bob Hartmann. You went out on a
limb for us -- I think it would have worked and worked well!
Bob was terribly disappointed. I realize that you were quite
ill while all of this was going on, and I think you should know
that we weren't even given the courtesy of a phone call from
Ron Nessen or Bob Meade telling us it had been cancelled.

I had hired a crew and sent my Associate Producer, Lee Hale,
to Washington to see that all went well. Bob Orben had written
a terrific spot, it was on cue cards, and it wasn't until the
morning of the day the spot was to be taped that we learned it
had been cancelled. Mr. Hale called to say that he would be
there about an hour and a half earlier to get the camera set-up,
and that was when he was told, "Oh, that's been cancelled", and
that, Bob, is all the information we could ever get out of that
office.

I just got through reading a helluva an article about you -- and
that is why I thought I would tell you what happened because
you certainly don't run your office that way.

Thanks again for trying. I hope that someday I will have the
opportunity of meeting you in person.

Kindest regards,

Greg Garrison
Producer
The Dean Martin Celebrity Roast

March 2, 1976

MEMORANDUM FOR: MR. RED CAVANEY

FROM: TERRY O'DONNELL

SUBJECT: <u>California Trip</u>

Red, Bob Hope has offered to let the President use his house while the President is in California.

Apparently, it is about 20-minutes from the Century Plaza Hotel, and I am sure that it wouldn't be very convenient. I just wanted you to know the offer exists in case it fits into your plans.

Judy Hope, his daughter-in-law who is on the Domestic Council, can serve as a point of contact.

Thank you.

cc: Mr. Jones
    Mr. Nicholson

Angeles to campaign for the Republican nomination, the Hopes asked them to stay at their home; when the offer was turned down, Dolores Hope sent a flower basket to the Fords' hotel with a note "Next time make it our house *please!*"

That summer Bob Hope, like Sammy Davis, Jr., before him, got to sleep in the Lincoln Bedroom. He sent a thank-you letter:

> *I really enjoyed my stay in the Lincoln suite. The room service was beautiful and as I said at the show, I'm up for adoption! Enjoyed our golf game up until the skies fell in. . . .*
>
> *I just want you to know that I'm not an uncommitted comedian. Your record should be acknowledged by this country. You've done a great job. Keep swinging!*

Sammy Davis, Jr., also had to pay for all the singing and dancing he'd done for Nixon. A memo between staffers Ron Nessen and Don Rumsfeld early in Ford's administration reports that "Sammy Davis, Jr., has phoned me several times" to invite the Fords to an upcoming performance. "He would also like to be invited to dinner at the White House the night before." Nessen recommends they decline both invitations. "Sammy Davis, Jr., is closely identified with former President Nixon. I don't think President Ford should form any public relationship with him."

Jackie Gleason, another old duffer and Nixonite, sought to buy his way into Ford's heart with gifts that included, according to an official thank-you note, a set of gold-plated irons, golf shoes and pewter cups. Phil Harris, a singer and legendary party hound, was among the many show-biz has-beens who also golfed with the president. Flip Wilson owed the president a pro bono performance after losing a bet on the eighteenth hole at Lake of the Woods Country Club. He paid him back by performing his Nurse Geraldine shtick at Ford's sixty-second birthday party. A subsequent invitation to Ford to appear on "The Flip Wilson Show" was politely declined.

Mr. and Mrs. Frank Jameson of Glendale, California—aka Eva Gabor and husband—were presumptuously ingratiating. Mr. Jameson would cable the White House from European jaunts with such promises as IF THE BOSS CAN USE A FOURTH AT BURNING TREE [the golf course] SATURDAY OR SUNDAY WILL PLAY TO A 21 INSTEAD OF NORMAL 20. He'd call to see if they could drop by the White House and "stick their heads in the door" on their way through Washington. In November 1975, Ford wrote to thank Jameson for the "nice letter" in which he had offered his and Eva's advice on how to campaign:

Eva Gabor shmoozes Ford.

The Beach Boys tour the White House with Susan Ford. Mike Love zens out.

"Well—if your friends won't tell you, who will? But seriously, I do appreciate your constructive suggestions and recommendations and promise to keep them in mind."

Even Daniel Boorstin was a Ford shmoozer. Having entered the sixties deploring the rise of celebrity, by the mid-seventies he was a celebrity himself, one of the country's best-known scholars and authors and archon of establishmentarian American history at the Smithsonian Institution. Early in his administration Ford invited Boorstin to intimate, off-the-record "stag" parties where a small group of advisors, cabinet members and bright outsiders kicked around ideas with the president. In November 1976 Ford appointed Boorstin Librarian of Congress despite rather intense opposition from professional librarians who thought one of their own should have the job, and from minority groups, including a group within the Library of Congress itself, who thought he was a reactionary and racist.

The Ford kids brought their favorite rock stars to the White House. Susan had the Beach Boys over. Steve introduced his dad to Peter Frampton. In addition to having unwittingly met a Beatle assassin, Ford was the first president to meet an actual Beatle. His son Jack had met George Harrison backstage after a concert and invited Harrison, who came along with Ravi Shankar, Billy Preston and entourage, to meet the president at the White House in December 1974. Harrison most likely lobbied Ford for the recovery of some $5 million in proceeds from his 1971 Concert for Bangladesh, which he'd intended to donate to UNICEF; most of it had been impounded by the Internal Revenue Service in 1972. Harrison and the president exchanged pins. The Beatle gave the president a pin with the Sanskrit om symbol on it; Ford gave Harrison a WIN button (which stood for Whip Inflation Now, a clumsy public-relations effort). Later that week the White House staff had to mend fences with the pouting Independent Cattlemen's Association, a powerful conservative lobby that

Ford was the first president to meet a Beatle (with Billy Preston and Ravi Shankar).

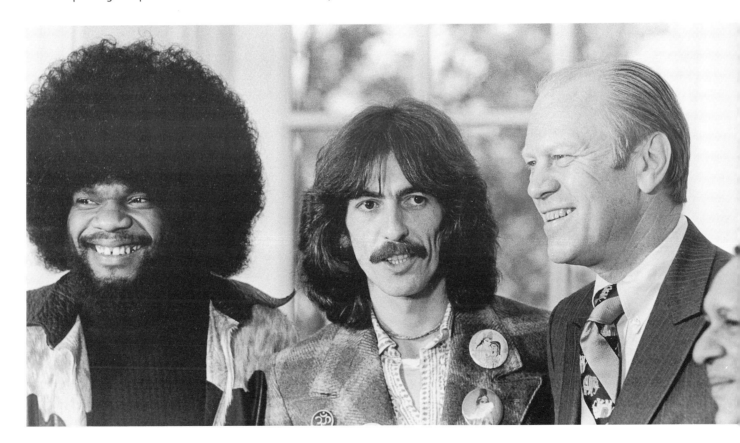

demanded to know how the president found time to meet with a Beatle on a day when he was too busy to meet with their delegation.

Despite all the partying, when the Fords looked to Hollywood for support in the 1976 elections they found the stars in a state of confusion over where their loyalties—and best interests—lay. Hollywood

Cesar Romero, Zsa Zsa Gabor, even the Maytag Repairman came out for Betty's party in Beverly Hills.

liberals were inclined to back Jerry Brown in the Democratic primary and later Jimmy Carter in the general election, though some feminists were great admirers of Betty Ford. Hollywood conservatives were even more confused over whether to back Ford or Ronald Reagan, who was running hard for the Republican nomination.

Hollywood gossip columnists had a field day pointing out who showed and who didn't at the Celebrities for President Ford party thrown for Betty at The Bistro in Beverly

Hills on May 6, 1976, the peak of the Ford-versus-Reagan primary battle. The event was organized by Mr. and Mrs. Glenn Ford. Cary Grant came as Betty's escort, and Dolores Hope and Eva Gabor led the guest list, which included Zsa Zsa Gabor, Sonny Bono, Freddie Prinze, Milton Berle, Red Buttons and his wife, Mr. and Mrs. Pat Boone, Ricardo Montalban, Ernest Borgnine and his wife, Mr. and Mrs. William Shatner, Elke Sommer, Marty Allen, Steve Lawrence and Edie Gorme, Joan Rivers, Art Linkletter, Tony Curtis, Jim

Opposite. *Steve and Edie clowned.*

Left. *Sonny wore his best suit.*

Nabors, Farrah Fawcett, Nanette Fabray, Xavier Cugat, Cesar Romero, Robert Conrad, Bert Convy, Jim Brown, Ray Bolger, Hugh O'Brian, Roger Miller, Connie Stevens and the Maytag Repairman. Nancy Sinatra and Helen Reddy, though Democrats in sympathy, showed up to pay their respects to Betty.

Ford's battle with Reagan persisted all the way through to the Republican convention at the Kansas City Convention Center that July. In the end Ford squeaked through with 1,187 delegates to Reagan's 1,070. The instant it was clear Ford had won, he went to Reagan's room and offered him the vice-presidential spot on the ticket. In his memoirs, he reports that Reagan's response was chilly. In a photo taken as they left the room and descended a staircase to appear together on the convention stage, Reagan, by his own admission a bad loser, looks to be entertaining the notion of Ford's taking one more of his famous tumbles down the flight of stairs.

MR. PEANUT

AND HIS GOLEM

How dreary to be Somebody!
How public like a Frog
To tell one's name the livelong June
To an admiring Bog!
Emily Dickinson

We've got the biggest star in television," a White House media advisor told Richard Schickel during the mid-seventies. "He is the first television President. He looks normal on television, natural; most of all he's *comfortable*."

Today it's hard to imagine he was talking about Jimmy Carter. But Jimmy Carter was, in fact, elected almost solely on the basis of his image. His achievements and experience were limited, but that was his strength—his negative capability, as it were. As Braudy notes in *The Frenzy of Renown,* the image Carter brought to the public's mind was a recurrent favorite of American politics and pop culture: the lone man, the outsider who rides in to clean up the corrupt town. He was Shane, he was Clint Eastwood; in four years Ronald Reagan would gallop into town, and in twelve more Bill Clinton. He was The Man from Plains, the plain man, the peanut farmer with a grin on his face and lust in his heart. If he had no substantial accomplishments to boast about, at least he had committed no crimes.

Four years later Carter was defeated by his image. While he was tinkering down in the boiler room of the government, Carter's image got away from him and escaped into the etheric zone of myth and media, where it taunted him like an evil golem.

Page 131. *Shirley Maclaine checks Jimmy's aura.*

133

Of all modern presidents, Jimmy Carter was the most inept manager of his own celebrity. He stupefied the nation by proceeding to look more accident-prone and do-nothing than even Gerald Ford. Despite some admirable accomplishments as president, he gave the impression of nearly catatonic inactivity. His record seemed to reflect nothing but a parade of demoralization and defeat, at the hands of the oil cartel, the Soviets, the Iranians, the Panamanians, his relatives, his friends, and the Killer Rabbit.

Every time Carter assayed an overtly symbolic gesture meant to correct his image, it was the wrong one. He seemed perversely blind to the bleakness of the messages he was sending. There was the unlit Christmas tree, the unheated White House, the boycotted Olympics, the Panama Canal give-away, the glum fireside scoldings, the yellow ribbons, and finally his brooding withdrawal into silence and solitude as the hostages languished in Tehran and his wife was out acting as his proxy on the campaign trail. In his way he made himself every bit as embarrassing as Nixon and Ford had been. He looked weak, emasculated, petulant, priggish, hogtied and helpless.

On becoming president, Carter underwent a disastrous version of the change Kennedy had experienced. It was one thing to be a candidate—to look better than Ford, to speak more plainly and seem more intelligent and upstanding—but it was another thing to be the president. It was the *impression* of failure, rather than failure itself, that was his unpardonable shortcoming. Celebrity is the aristocracy of democratic America, attained not through birth and blood but the good will and interest of the audience.

Above. *Marcel Marceau mugs; Amy looks bored.*

Opposite. *Unlike JFK, Carter was willing to wear a funny hat—this one provided by character actor–spokesman Iron Eyes Cody.*

There is no gift dearer to Americans, no power more cherished than the ability to bestow upon an average citizen—one of us—fame and social status. It is the essence of the American Dream, the defining genius of democracy as a self-policing social system: the core belief, however illusory, that we choose our famous and powerful from our own ranks, and the associated hope, however faint, that any one of us may be a winner in this lottery of success.

This is the crucial aspect of "empty celebrity" misapprehended in elitist social ideologies like Daniel Boorstin's. In America, celebrity *must be* empty, or very nearly so, to allow us to fill it with our fantasies, dreams and desires. This is why so many Hollywood stars, pop singers and politicians are mediocre at best. They are our representatives in Hollywood and in Washington—*they represent us.* And because of this close identification, we're willing to forgive much.

The one thing we insist is that they have the good grace to value the gift we've given them. We demand that they love us back. It's one thing if they can't manage the pressure of the job, but it's something else entirely if they can't manage the pressure of public attention and admiration. This is a form of rejection we do not tolerate, whether it is

Sally Struthers jumps for joy.

from presidents or pop stars. Nothing prompts the public to revoke the gift more surely than an inability or refusal to fulfill the ceremonial role as our aristocracy.

Jimmy Carter's unpardonable sin was not his failure on the managerial level. As an executive he was not all that incompetent, and his successor irrefutably demonstrated how high our tolerance is for managerial ineptitude. Carter's sin was that he did not seem to appreciate the gift. He did not love us back. He hid from us and refused to play the role: he was an ingrate.

The arrogance of this was particularly stinging given the appealing public image of humble servitude he had originally presented. During the campaign of 1976, he had struck Gerald Ford as "an outsider with little more going for him than a winning smile. . . . His self-confidence . . . came very close to arrogance." As a fellow politician, Ford had seen something it took the rest of us a few more years to recognize. In the White House, Carter's arrogance soured into the bitter self-absorption of the sanctimonious preacher caught with his pants down who, in accepting his guilt, damns everyone else.

Even the pope seemed more at home in the White House than the Carters.

✦ ✦ ✦

Carter was, after all, a sometime preacher and a Born Again. He knew himself to be a sinner and he knew himself to be unworthy. "He seemed hushed and pinched with reverence for his own success," Schickel writes. "The sourness and the whininess [kept] coming through. And the provinciality. His Southernness, therefore his 'otherness' for most Americans, kept coming through." If you were to sum up the impression Carter made as president, Schickel says, it would be one of "piety, careerism and a darkling soul."

Part of Carter's self-consciousness seems to have resulted from the touchiness peculiar to some Southerners who reach the national stage. In his memoirs, *Keeping Faith*, Carter complains:

> *Before we arrived in Washington, some of the society-page writers were deploring the prospective dearth of social grace in the White House and predicting four years of nothing but hillbilly music, and ignorant Bible-toting Southerners trying to reimpose Prohibition in the capital city. The local cartoonists had a field day characterizing us as barefoot country hicks with straw sticking out of our ears, clad in overalls and unfamiliar with the proper use of indoor plumbing. I recall a full page cartoon depicting an outhouse on the White House lawn, with my mother wearing a sunbonnet and smoking a corncob pipe.*

Rosalynn had her own problems with the press. In *First Lady from Plains* she recalls that her poor press image was

> *an annoyance that just wouldn't go away. I thought that if I were working productively and accomplishing something worthwhile, the image would take care of itself. Wrong. I learned that labels are easy to come by and hard to overcome. I had been called a "steel magnolia" in the campaign, to which I didn't object, and it was just as well ... [because] "steel magnolia" is in print forever. And by the end of our first year in Washington I found myself described as being "fuzzy"— which is better than having a bad image, but not as good as a good one!*

Shirley Maclaine making a very close check of the president's aura.

She also complains,

Before Jimmy's inauguration, the press had painted us as country farm people who would bring gingham and square dances to the White House. We did. Sometimes. But we also brought a parade of America's greatest classical talent and some of the most elegant events ever held at the White House.

Rosalynn goes on to list various classical performers she and Jimmy had invited to the White House, many of whom had been regulars there since Jacqueline Kennedy made it an "oasis of culture" in America—Beverly Sills, Leontyne Price, Mikhail Baryshnikov, Pavarotti and the like. She doesn't seem to understand why their standard black-tie affairs were unconvincing, why they looked exactly like self-conscious, hobnobbing philistinism. Unfortunately, she and Jimmy just did not look natural sitting at the feet of

Betty Davis looks askance.

Somehow, the Carters never looked comfortable in the White House "oasis of culture."

Rudolf Serkin. They looked like a small-town couple on their best behavior, trying to prove with their rigid attentiveness that they could appreciate serious music. The back-lawn barbecues for the year's leading NASCAR drivers, with Rosalynn on stage singing with Willie Nelson—how could these not be more convincing?

The embrace of populist culture had, after all, been the theme of Carter's winning campaign. Beyond defining his image, it had brought a political expediency at a time when changes in campaign contribution disclosure rules were

making it difficult for individuals to become major supporters. The challenge now was to induce large numbers of people to contribute funds in small amounts. Carter's 1976 campaign was the first to experiment with pop-music concerts as fund raisers. As it turned out, the events were only moderately successful cash cows but all too successful in forging an indelible association with country rock bands such as The Allman Brothers, Black Oak Arkansas and the Marshall Tucker Band. Carter never was able to shake the resulting redneck

Embracing populist culture was a political expediency, but it helped define the Carter image. Jimmy poses with Crosby, Stills, and Nash (above) and the Bee Gees (opposite); Rosalynn with Waylon Jennings.

stigma this association produced. Reagan and Bush's media organizers were able to use this fund-raising tactic more successfully; Clinton's absolutely depended on it to save his campaign.

Even so, Carter's countryfied populism inspired some of the most memorable and likable cultural events at the White House, such as a blues and jazz festival on the White House lawn. Numerous country stars played and stayed at the Carter White House, including Waylon Jennings, June Carter and Johnny Cash, Emmy Lou Harris and Loretta Lynn, who later telegrammed, DEAR ROSALYNN, I'VE BEEN ON THE ROAD EVER SINCE

LAST WEEK AND I JUST AIN'T HAD TIME TO THANK YOU AND JIMMY FOR INVITING ME AND DOOLITTLE TO THE WHITE HOUSE.

Willie Nelson was the country-music star most closely identified with the Carters. He visited several times, and he caused a small scandal when a rumor spread that he'd gone up on the White House roof, where Jimmy kept an amateur astronomer's telescope, to smoke some pot. After Willie played at the reception for the NASCAR drivers, Jimmy wrote him, "Nothing of lesser magnitude than the Camp David Summit would have prevented me from welcoming you and Connie and the band to the White House personally."

But there was only so much down-home charm Carter could borrow from Willie or Loretta. Ultimately he looked just as stiff with them, his big grin just as forced and panicky, as he did when hobnobbing with representatives of higher culture, one of whom was Andy Warhol. They made an absurd pair. The calculated motivation for bringing their radically different orbits into conjunction was just too blatantly careerist. They had nothing in common but what they thought they could get from each other.

In his memoirs, *Holy Terror*, Warhol biographer Bob Colacello recalls that Andy and Jimmy Carter met in 1976, when Andy traveled to Plains to do his portrait for the cover of the Sunday *New York Times Magazine*, which ran an article on him by Norman Mailer. Warhol reported back to Colacello that Rosalynn was "the tough one" in the family. "She wears the pantsuit. Polyester." Warhol was both fascinated and horrified by the family—the bible-thumping sister, bubba Billy (later named by *Esquire* magazine as

Another link in The King chain: a pre-presidential snapshot, backstage in Atlanta.

Willie Nelson at the White House with Emmy Lou Harris.

"Primate of the Decade") and the wacky Miz Lillian, who "kept saying that she looked like me. She sort of does. It was too nutty."

Andy nevertheless made a show of supporting Jimmy, and Jimmy made a show of accepting the support. Warhol donated prints of his Carter portrait to the inaugural fund and to the Democratic National Committee and gave Chip Carter a subscription to *Interview*—an unusual gesture for the notoriously thrifty artist. Colacello claims that Andy was buttering up the Carters as an attempt to protect his relationship with the Shah of Iran, a big patron of his and his entrée to the international jet set and royalty. Andy figured, Colacello reported, that establishing a relationship with the Carters would "get the art world intellectuals and the liberals in the press off our backs" about associating with such unpopular figures as the Shah and Imelda Marcos. Still, he declined an invitation to Carter's inauguration, Colacello says, preferring instead to attend the opening of the "Cats and Dogs Show" in Kuwait.

When Andy and Colacello finally did visit the White House one afternoon, Andy passed by the president's secretary eating lunch at her desk. Colacello writes, " 'Gee,' " said Andy, " 'here we are in the President's office, Bob, and the secretary is eating the same smelly tuna fish sandwich that they eat in every office, with the same smelly pickle.' "

In the Oval Office, Carter and Andy were shy with each other to the point of near speechlessness. "In fairness to Andy, it must be said that Carter was almost as awkward as he was," Colacello recalls. " 'He's no Nelson Rockefeller' was the way Andy put it later."

✦   ✦   ✦

Stiffness and diffidence marked Carter's meetings with all kinds of visitors, from celebrities to foreign dignitaries to delegations of party hacks from back home. Like Kennedy, he restricted the official White House photographers access, generally eschewing candid or intimate shots in favor of formal "grip 'n' grin" sessions. They produced uncomfortably posed That's-Me-with-the-President photos that party hacks could take home to hang in their offices and barber shops, but that were of little use in giving the public at large the sense that they had a friend in the White House. Rock stars and movie stars and the pope, when visiting the Carter White House, looked more at ease there than he did. Only

Jimmy and Andy.

*Amy's favorite celebrities—
including John Travolta,
Mickey Mouse, and Benji the
Wonder Dog—tried to help her
overcome her shyness.*

Amy Carter looked more excruciatingly shy than her father, even when the guests were her favorite celebrities—John Travolta, whom she asked be invited for her birthday, Mickey Mouse, the Campbell Soup Kids, Benji the Wonder Dog.

Jimmy simply was not blessed with the gift of *lightness.* He turned everything into an academic lecture, or worse, a sermon. When Cher once asked the president if there was any message he would like her to convey to the public on her next "Tonight Show" appearance, she received a two-page telegram full of suggestions. It's difficult to imagine Cher turning to Johnny and saying, "You know, we've all heard quite a bit recently about the troubles of Washington, D.C. But one of the most encouraging signs of a new spirit in our country is the way the capital is becoming a showplace for the nation. There's the beautiful, modern Metro system which partly opened last year and soon will be expanded. And crime in Washington has fallen sharply, in comparison to other cities. . . ."

Bob Hope was ever present, of course, at least up through 1978. But with anti-Shah Iranian students demonstrating all over the United States, by the following year he was firing off telegram lectures like:

DEAR MR PRESIDENT . . . ARE WE GOING TO STAND FOR THESE KIND OF PEOPLE TEARING UP OUR PROPERTY AND INSULTING US THIS WAY STOP PLEASE DO SOMETHING TO DEPART THESE TERRORISTS

BOB HOPE

Please do something—please do something to depart—by the final year, the whole nation was yelling it at him. Even Rosalynn was begging it of him. Rosalynn Carter did virtually all the campaigning for her husband in 1980, while he all but disappeared inside the White House, allegedly absorbed in negotiating the release of the hostages in Iran. She recalls what it was like taking the heat for him in public:

As the campaign and the situation in Iran wore on, I . . . had to counter accusations from our political opponents and the press that Jimmy was "hiding in the Rose Garden" or even, as one ludicrous rumor had it, having a nervous breakdown. . . . Typically, in an interview for an Italian television reporter, the first question was: "The Pre-see-dent, when come he out of the Rose Gar-deen?!" I wanted to tell her that he was very busy that day in the Rose Gar-deen, thank you!

The questions on the campaign trail changed from "What's the President doing about the hostage situation?" to "Why doesn't he do something?" . . . Each week I rushed home after my last appearance, praying that a miracle had happened and that there would be some word of encouragement—invariably to be disappointed.

There were always negotiations, always plans that "just might work," and constant pressure upon Jimmy to take drastic action, and instead of giving moral support to him in a difficult situation, I'm afraid I was sometimes guilty of adding

Hope scolded Carter over the hostage crisis; after that, Carter was without hope.

to the pressure. Each time I wanted him to "do something—anything," he usually would calmly say, "Like what? What else do you want me to do?"

"Couldn't you mine the harbors?" I would ask. . . .

His reply to her, to everyone, was much like his response to Hope's telegram:

Thank you for sharing your concern about Iranian protestors in this country. I appreciate knowing your views.

Sincerely,
Jimmy Carter

In the end, Jimmy Carter looked like he didn't want to go on being president any more than the public wanted him to. It explains his swift, preemptive concession speech the night Ronald Reagan trounced him. He was so relieved he resigned before we finished voting him out.

There was indeed something of the Born Again spirit in it: he had sinned, and he had taken his punishment. Now he was eager to enjoy his presidential afterlife, which he clearly has. He is indisputably the happiest, healthiest, most well-adjusted and productive ex-president in living memory. Not unlike Truman, who also fled the White House with undisguised relief, Jimmy Carter's reputation as president really only blossomed once his presidency actually ended. As the Christian life on earth is a trial to be endured before eternal joy in heaven, Carter's term seems to have been the necessary prelude to a much happier life as ex-president.

HOLLYWOOD EAST

For years, I've heard the question:
"How could an actor be president?"
I've sometimes wondered how you could be
president and not be an actor.
Ronald Reagan

We choose the leader who best suits our group fantasy at the time," psychohistorian Lloyd deMause says. That's why most leaders "have no personal values. They just follow whatever irrational wishes we want to pour into them. So you'll get a wide range of personalities who will become these delegates or toadies of the people when the country is in the mood for irrational activities."

Enter Ronald Reagan.

He was, in many ways, the apotheosis of Kennedy. With JFK, America had had a president who became a tv star; now it had elected a tv star president. Reagan was the fulfillment of conservative Daniel Boorstin's worst nightmare: a truly empty celebrity in the White House.

In a sense he was the antipode to Jimmy Carter. Whereas Carter was all work and no ceremony, Ronald Reagan was a purely ceremonial president. Whereas Carter had been an aloof and self-righteous intellectual, Reagan was amiably low-brow, downright cuddly and, like any Hollywood careerist who never managed to climb beyond the middle rungs of the ladder, an inveterate ingratiating shmoozer.

Page 153. *Reagan with Christie Brinkley, Cheryl Tiegs, Nancy, and Brooke Shields.*

Reagan, a pop-culture creation, looked more populist than Carter ever had—even at the Grand Ole Opry with Roy Acuff.

To liberals and sophisticates, Reagan's enormous popularity was incontrovertible proof of how ignorant the populace was, how easily duped it could be by idealistic images, how the televisions people never turned off had destroyed their ability to discern fact from fantasy. Perhaps the truth, however, is that the public didn't want a "real" president anymore, at least not just then. America had had strong-willed, professional politicians in LBJ and Richard Nixon and a workaholic micromanager in Carter. Maybe Americans had simply had their fill of glum reality.

Now they were going to the movies.

Opposite. A chorus line: hoofing with Shirley Jones and Marvin Hamlisch, who wrote the music for Reagan's theme song.

"No presidency has been more image conscious or image driven than that of Ronald Reagan," Hedrick Smith maintains in *The Power Game*. "During the Reagan era, Washington began calling itself 'Hollywood East,' exulting in celebrity politics." And if there was any single hallmark of Reagan's presidency, it was his proclivity to mingle fantasy and reality, real life and the movies. Almost all of Reagan's most successful lines were taken from movies. "I am paying for this microphone, Mr. Breen," was the line he used to crush George Bush in the 1980 New Hampshire primary debate. He later speculated, "I may have won the debate, the primary—and the nomination—right there." It was a line paraphrased from the 1948 Frank Capra movie *State of the Union*. He appropriated

Above. *Wayne Newton doing his Robert Goulet impression. Note the foreign guests' mystified looks.*

```
  12
       2136502444 TDRN HOLLYWOOD CA 4 10-28 0829P EST
  13
⌣ 14  MS PRESIDENT RONALD REAGON, DLR
  15
      WHITE HOUSE DC
  16
⌣ 17  DEAR MR PRESIDENT;
  18
  19
⌣ 20  YEAH....
  21
  22     FRANCIS ALBERT  SINATRA
⌣ 23
  24
  ..  2032 EST
```

Opposite. *Sinatra was rumored to be back-dooring the president in the White House.*

The president as pop star—with a bullet. John Hinckley, Jr., trying to impress another pop icon (Jodie Foster), aimed his pop gun at Reagan.

Clint Eastwood's "Make my day," and the day he was shot he quipped, "Honey, I forgot to duck," a Jack Demspey line, and "All in all, I'd rather be in Philadelphia," a line from W. C. Fields.

In his revised, postpresidential memoirs, *An American Life*, Reagan reports his dad remarked the day he was born, "He looks like a fat little Dutchman. But who knows, he might grow up to be president some day." *Where's the Rest of Me?*, published in the mid-1960s, gave the same scene a different twist: "The story begins with a close-up of a bottom" is the first line of the book. It's baby Reagan's bottom being slapped by the doctor at birth. "My face was blue from screaming," he goes on, "my bottom was red from whacking, and my father claimed afterward that he was white."

Remembering the lead soldiers he had as a kid, Reagan writes in *An American Life*, "To this day I get a little thrill out of seeing a cabinet full of toy soldiers." The ease with which he walked away from all those marines spilled out of their toybox in

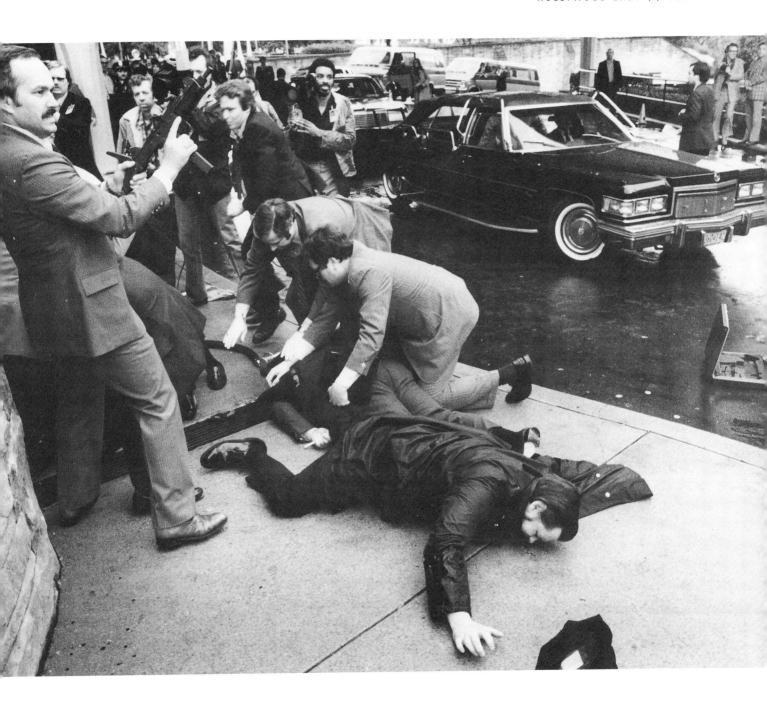

Superman sweats; Frank Gifford models leisure wear.

Right. *Stallone looks like he's considering his own run for the presidency.*

Opposite. *Group portrait with Cher's hair, Tom Cruise, and Bruce Jenner.*

Lebanon comes to mind. When as a young man Reagan decided to become a radio sports announcer, he did so because, he says, he'd seen movies in which sports announcers played themselves and figured that radio could be his stepping stone to Hollywood. Auditioning for his first announcing job, he gave a pretend play-by-play of a high school game he'd been in, but for his reenactment he put himself in the game-winning role. As a professional announcer, he worked from a ticker tape and embellished its information with visual details

from his imagination. Reagan once announced a University of Michigan game in which Gerald Ford played center. Years later, according to Hedrick Smith, he was asked if he would have preferred to broadcast live, rather than from ticker tape. " 'Oh, no,' Reagan shook his head, 'you see, the thing about doing it from the wire was that you could create the scene on your own.' "

During his first week in Hollywood Reagan recalls that he felt as though he were starring in a movie called *The Remaking of Dutch Reagan.* The wardrobe

Opposite and below. *The Gipper killing time in the Oval Office.*

Left. *Reagan looks up to Patrick Ewing.*

department almost flunked him because they said his head was too small for his shoulders. "See what you can do about his head," his casting director demanded.

Reagan narrated films during World War Two that faked aerial shots of Tokyo using a miniature city built by Hollywood set creators. Years later, as governor of California, when he flew in for a visit to the real Tokyo he reminisced, "I couldn't help but think of the huge model of Tokyo that we'd made secretly during the war."

Movie footage was as close as he got to the war, though in later years he seemed to forget that. In *An American Life* he recalls being shocked and moved by footage shot inside liberated concentration camps. As president, Reagan told Israeli Prime Minister Yitzhak Rabin that he'd actually been a photographer there himself.

Reagan met Nancy Davis, who was to become his First Lady, in the late 1940s, through a case of mistaken identity. She was a young actress, he remembers, "extremely upset

Nancy explaining jelly beans to a young visitor.

Mr. T plays Santa for Nancy.

Henry Kissinger tried to look dopier than his president.

because the name of another actress identified as Nancy Davis had appeared on the membership rosters of several Communist front groups and she was receiving notices of their meetings in her mail. . . . " As president of the Screen Actors Guild, Reagan did a little research and cleared her.

When he ran for the California governorship in 1966, his opponent Pat Brown made a tv commercial in which he told a group of children, "I'm running against an actor, and you know who killed Abe Lincoln, don't you?" Gene Kelly taped an ad in which he said, "Hello, I'm Gene Kelly, professional actor. I've played many roles before the camera. I've been a soldier, a gambler and even a major league baseball player. I know I could play the role of a governor, but that I could never really sit in his chair and make decisions affecting the education of millions of children."

Nobody bought the insinuations and Reagan handily defeated Brown. "Being an actor who was running for political office wasn't all drawbacks," Reagan opines. "Many people develop an affection and feelings of friendship for someone they enjoy on the screen, and that could be an advantage for me."

Even Reagan's first run at the presidency was a strange mix of fact and fantasy. In 1968, California Republicans requested he allow them to list his name on the ballot as a favorite son in the primary election. He remembers they persuaded him by telling him, "A favorite son candidate is not the same thing as a *real* candidate. . . ." When people told him how happy they were to see him run, he kept insisting ". . . but I'm not *running* for president." They'd reply that "we're going to consider you a real candidate and campaign on that basis." And he'd say, "I'll have to repudiate you on that—I'm not a *real* candidate." "We know that," they'd say, "but we're going to do it anyway."

Reagan's ability to see fantasy and fact simultaneously may have been a kind of double vision. He has mentioned "a trick with my contact lenses that helped me see not only my notes and the teleprompter but everything else in life." As a nearsighted actor, he was one of the first Americans to wear contact lenses. He recalls,

> *I discovered that if I wore only one lens, nature sort of took over and, in effect, gave me bifocals. I wear a contact lens on my left eye but nothing over my right eye; the corrective lens over my left eye gives me 20-20 vision for seeing things over distances, while my right eye takes over at shorter range and allows me to read fine print. Everything is in balance, equalized by nature.*

One tv critic thought a Walter Cronkite presidency would be the logical next step after Reagan's.

✦   ✦   ✦

Much of the Reagan administration's methodology for handling media and press came directly out of the "textbook" developed for Nixon by public-relations staffers like H. R. Haldeman and David Gergen. Half of Reagan's media team were old Nixon hands, including Gergen (who, like Roger Ailes, would later make the transition to the other side of the camera as a media personality and expert commentator). The other half were old Reagan hands like Mike ("the vicar of visuals") Deaver, well accustomed to producing and directing Reagan.

Intensifying Nixon's strategy, Reagan's handlers restricted media access to the president more severely than ever before. Reagan held a fraction of the press conferences previous presidents had. His few speaking appearances before the public were meticulously scripted and rehearsed, with their air time synchronized for optimum tv coverage. The Reagan media machine erred only when it strayed from the script—and usually it was Reagan whose lips and mind did the straying. The best-known incident was a classic example of Reagan's goofy playfulness: during a pre-show radio sound check he announced, "My fellow Americans, I am pleased to tell you I just signed legislation which outlaws Russia forever. The bombing begins in five minutes."

There were times when his handlers rehearsed him so mercilessly they literally overloaded his brain. In his first debate with Fritz Mondale in 1984, exhausted from days of grueling rehearsal and oversaturated with data incomprehensible to him, he mentally collapsed on camera and babbled random facts and figures in an alarmingly convincing display of senility. "I nearly blew the whole race," he admits in his memoirs. ". . . I think I was just overtrained . . . I don't think anybody could have retained all the things pumped into my brain during the days leading up to the debate; I goofed a couple of times." His handlers meant well, he concedes, but "they fill your head with all sorts of details, technicalities, and statistics . . . you just can't command all that information. . . ."

As was typical of him, Reagan recovered in the second debate with a well-timed one-liner.

The Reagans stand at attention as the pope descends from the heavens.

Michael Jackson was undoubtedly the most regally attired visitor to the Reagan White House. That didn't stop Reagan's cabinet from joking around with the glove he left behind.

Reagan in his head-thrown-back pose, with actor Fess Parker at a ballgame (above) and with a silly teen queen (opposite).

While doing their best to control what the president said, Reagan's people flooded the world with his image. Compared to John Kennedy's 35,000 official photographs, the Reagan library holds 1,500,000 photographs, 24,000 video-tapes, and 25,000 audiotapes, as well as vaults of film. In Nixon's day, Haldeman had ruled that a good picture says more than a thousand words every time. And Haldeman had been saddled with one of the least photogenic presidents in recent history. With Reagan, Deaver and his crew had a president capable of little else *but* posing for cameras.

The hundreds of prints in the Reagan Library photo archives show him running through endless repetitions of a very small repertoire of poses: the hearty head-thrown-back guffaw; the slightly dazed, slightly goofy aw-shucks grin; the lips-pursed, chin-dropped look that signaled seriousness, sadness or anger. It is the instinctive, mindless body-think of anonymous fashion models in department store advertisements, and it had the effect of reducing him to a mannequin. The most polished of presidential photos, they are also the least interesting. Posed with other actors or models, Reagan fades into the group; posed with more ordinary people, he looks like a life-size cutout.

In *First and Last Emperors*, Canadian scholars Kenneth Dean and Brian Massumi examine the symbolism and iconography of Reagan's imagery and find curious archaic parallels. Two hundred years before the Christian era, a warlord in China named Qin Shi Huangdi proclaimed himself emperor and established what became a model for abso-

lutist imperial states to come. In order to be obeyed as the absolute ruler, the emperor disappeared as a mortal and commanded that his image, godlike and eternal, be reproduced throughout the empire. While he hid inside the imperial palace, the empire became his body. He spread his body out: the palace was his heart, the roads his veins and arteries, the army his feet, the Great Wall his skin, the laws and proclamations he had ordered be inscribed everywhere his voice. Though the emperor was invisible, he was represented in full throughout the empire. When he died, he disappeared deeper into the empire, buried in a secret tomb that replicated the whole empire in miniature, walled in and guarded by an army of terra-cotta soldiers.

Some 2,200 years later, Ronald Reagan visited the First Emperor's excavated tomb. He joked about wishing for a Great Wall around the White House and posed behind a headless terra-cotta soldier, placing his own head in the empty space where the soldier's clay head would have been. "Reagan," Dean and Massumi dryly observe, "was never more serious than when he was joking."

They note that in *King's Row*—one of the very few films in which he played a bad guy—he utters the line "Where is the rest of me?" when he wakes up and discovers that a vengeful doctor has amputated his legs. In their book they reproduce doodles Reagan made while he sat, bored and dozing, during technical staff discussions; he drew himself without hands and feet.

Where was the rest of him? Spread out all over the place. A popular image at the height of his empire was of the Statue of Liberty wearing his head. The 1984 Republican convention presented the deeply unsettling vision of Reagan's enormous video image looming over real-life Nancy. Tiny, human Nancy waved up to that huge, ghostly image of her husband, and he waved back from the screen as though from the beyond.

Over the course of his reign Reagan, like the First Emperor, gradually disappeared physically. It was almost as though he were discarding body parts. He feigned laryngitis when he didn't want to speak to reporters, pleaded hearing-aid failure when he didn't want to hear their questions. There was the skin cancer they kept scraping off his nose, and the *New York Times* illustration explaining his prostate operation that made it look like his penis had fallen off.

When he had left the White House, strange photos of him appeared in the news after doctors drained water from his brain. Half his head was shaved and the other half bushy-haired; it looked like trick photography. (See what you can do about his head.)

Throughout his second term he seemed rarely to be in the White House, and when he was there he was napping. When he wasn't napping, he seemed to be in a waking dream state, his mind disappearing almost completely into movie fantasies.

While the real Reagan disappeared, his image kept appearing all over the world. In a very literal sense, Dean and Massumi argue, he became his own symbol, vanishing into his own empty and flat surface image, multiplied endlessly like a video loop.

By his second term those images, ubiquitously reproduced, began to make his tenure seem eternal. He was the first president in the memory of many Americans to have survived two full terms, and the notion of his going for a third, trial marketed by supporters, was not poorly received. There was an ageless quality to Reagan, a sense of America having become unmoored from time, a perception of his image, all at once youthfully gay and as old as a Komodo dragon, floating in a haze of postmodern hyperreality. There was no sense that America was going either forward or backward, no sense of motion at all. If, as Norman Mailer had forecast, Kennedy's presidency was a national soap opera, then Reagan's was a national sitcom. Not in its first prime-time run, but in a steady state of syndicated rerun, like "M*A*S*H" or "Cheers" or "The Honeymooners," appearing weeknights at odd hours on various channels and seeming to have been on forever, a kind of ritual permanence of daily life.

The immutability of Reagan's omnipresent image explains much about his curious power over the hearts and minds of so many people. Because it never appeared to change, his image produced an instantaneous nostalgia, the enemy of history.

Ronald Reagan took celebrity presidency the furthest it has yet been. Pure image, pure icon, pure symbol, he was not so much America's leader as he was its logo.

EPILOGUE

*The medium is the massage
and the masseur gets the votes.*
Joe McGinnis

The Bush-versus-Dukakis campaigns of 1988 brought the Nixonian style of television electioneering to its nadir. Both sides stumped entirely in images and monosyllabic bumper sticker slogans. It was sound-bite democracy. Television news reported the campaigns in the shortest sound bites ever, averaging 9.8 seconds. Often these reports didn't even amount to true sound bites, since the candidates themselves were not heard but only the reporters' voice-overs.

Whenever President Bush did speak for himself it always seemed to come out mush—what the *International Herald Tribune* called "nonwords." Not newspeak, but nospeak. At the advice of his handlers he began to simplify his sentences—and soon his speech was reduced to clipped, meaningless phrases lacking subject or verb. He tried literally wrapping himself in the flag at a flag factory, but proved himself far less adroit with the symbolic gestures that had been the trademark of his larger-than-life predecessor. Dukakis, unmindful of any of the lessons of JFK's media success, donned an ill-fitting helmet and rode around in an army tank, resembling a bobble-headed car toy.

179

Attempts by media advisors to quarantine the extraordinarily foolish candidate Dan Quayle were so desperate they became a story in themselves. Quayle was eventually forced to call a press conference to announce: "The so-called handlers story, part of it's true. But there will be no more handlers stories, because I'm the handler and I'll do the spinning. . . . I'm Doctor Spin, and I want you all to report that."

Lower than this, tv politics could not go.

At the shining moment of Bush's presidency, the Gulf War, in an attempt to repeat Reagan's winning image formulas, Bush too disseminated an endless video loop. This time, though, the image was not of Bush but of his Desert Storm surrogate, a smart bomb plummeting down a chimney in Iraq, and then the screen going blank. That blank tv screen was Bush's triumph and his vanishing, all at once, into a black hole from which he never reemerged.

The 1992 campaign marked a change in American politics. Bush's major opponents circumvented the network news and sound-bite politics by using alternative communication vehicles: Jerry Brown established a clever but failed toll-free 800-telephone line and billionaire Ross Perot bought his own seemingly limitless air time. However, the campaign's real departure came in the spring of 1992, when in a desperate but savvy act, Bill Clinton clasped Elvis' ghost to his bosom. Whereas Nixon had leerily touched The King's hand at arm's length, Clinton determined that he would *become* The King, the first publicly proclaimed Elvis impersonator in the White House.

Unimpressive as a personality, unconvincing as a politician, Clinton triumphed as the pop-culture candidate. As Bush became increasingly aloof, Clinton declared to the American people that their pop culture was his pop culture. There was MTV ("Gosh, this set is cool.") and "Heartbreak Hotel," there was Fleetwood Mac and his brother Roger's band, there was Michael Jackson, Diana Ross, Lou Reed, Goldie Hawn, Elton John, Chuck Berry, Kenny Rogers, the Grateful Dead, Michael Bolton, Don Henley, and on and on.

Although the faithful among the press found it all dazzling, "jaw-dropping," as *Entertainment Weekly* put it, Clinton's campaign was nothing more than a mélange of techniques used by every president since JFK—all those the forty-something Clinton and his media team had ever personally witnessed. And before his first hundred days had passed, Clinton brought David Gergen, architect of Nixonian image manipulation, into his White House as counsel. If anything was new, it was the avidity with which Clinton pursued his celebrity connections, the way he readily abandoned the last vestiges of presidential propriety as he immersed himself in the world of stars. As the Clintons moved into the White House, they brought a host of celebrities with them: Billy Crystal and Judy Collins, Liza Minnelli and Christopher Reeve; record industry mogul David Geffen offered advice on economic matters. At formal White House dinners, the stars at Clinton's elbow changed with every course; Barbra Streisand with the appetizers, Whoopi Goldberg at dessert.

But this is to be expected of an American president grasping for legitimacy in the eyes of a public willingly bombarded with celebrity fantasy worlds for the last half century. American culture *is* popular culture. Popularity *is* power. And Elvis has definitely *not* left the building.

BIBLIOGRAPHY

Adatto, Kiku. *Picture Perfect.* New York: Basic Books, 1993.

Barron, James. "Nixon Is 80 (And Elvis Joins Party)," *New York Times,* 10 January 1993.

Blonsky, Marshall. *American Mythologies.* New York: Oxford University Press, 1992.

Boorstin, Daniel J. *The Image.* New York: Atheneum, 1987.

Braudy, Leo. *The Frenzy of Renown.* New York: Oxford University Press, 1986.

Brownstein, Ronald. *The Power and The Glitter.* New York: Pantheon, 1990.

Califano, Joseph A., Jr. *The Triumph and Tragedy of Lyndon Johnson.* New York: Simon and Schuster, 1991.

Carter, Jimmy. *Keeping Faith.* New York: Bantam, 1982.

Carter, Rosalynn. *First Lady from Plains.* New York: Houghton Mifflin, 1984.

Colacello, Bob. *Holy Terror.* New York: HarperCollins, 1990.

Collier, Peter, and David Horowitz. *The Kennedys.* New York: Simon and Schuster, 1984.

Dean, Kenneth, and Brian Massumi. *First and Last Emperors.* New York: Autonomedia, 1992.

DeMause, Lloyd. *Foundations of Psychohistory.* New York: Creative Roots, 1982.

Ford, Gerald. *A Time to Heal.* New York: Harper and Row, 1979.

Gilbert, Robert. *The Mortal Presidency.* New York: Basic Books, 1993.

Hall, Gordon Langley, and Ann Pinchot. *Jacqueline Kennedy.* New York: Signet, 1964.

Hersh, Seymour M. "Nixon's Last Cover-Up: The Tapes He Wants the Archives to Suppress," *The New Yorker,* 14 December 1992.

Hopkins, Jerry. *Elvis: The Final Years.* New York: St. Martin's, 1980.

Johnson, Lady Bird. *A White House Diary.* New York: Holt, Rinehart and Winston, 1970.

Johnson, Lyndon Baines. *The Vantage Point.* New York: Holt, Rinehart and Winston, 1971.

Mailer, Norman. "Superman Comes to the Supermart," *Esquire,* November 1960.

McGinnis, Joe. *The Selling of the President 1968.* New York: Trident, 1969.

Nixon, Richard. *RN.* New York: Grosset and Dunlap, 1975.

O'Donnell, Kenneth P., and David F. Powers. *Johnny, We Hardly Knew Ye.* Boston: Little, Brown, 1970.

Reagan, Ronald. *An American Life.* New York: Simon and Schuster, 1990.

Schickel, Richard. *Intimate Strangers: The Cult of Celebrity.* New York: Doubleday, 1985.

Smith, Hedrick. *The Power Game.* New York: Random House, 1988.

Trow, George W. S. *Within the Context of No Context.* Boston: Little, Brown, 1981.

White, Theodore H. *The Making of the President 1960.* New York: Atheneum, 1961.

Wyatt, Clarence R. *Paper Soldiers.* New York: W. W. Norton, 1993.